Somerset

Born,

Somerset

Bred

Roger Evans

COUNTRYSIDE BOOKS
NEWBURY BERKSHIRE

COUNTRYSIDE BOOKS
3 Catherine Road
Newbury, Berkshire

To view our complete range of books
please visit us at
www.countrysidebooks.co.uk

ISBN 978 1 84674 260 6

Cover designed by Peter Davies,
Nautilus Design

Produced through MRM Associates Ltd., Reading
Typeset by Mac Style, Beverley, East Yorkshire
Printed by Information Press, Oxford

Contents

Foreword

Knocking on Evans' door

The knock on the front door was closely followed by the click of its handle and a female voice declaring, 'Coo-ee, Mrs Evans. It's only me!' By the time my mother had said, 'Come on in', 'Only Me' was already standing there with her hand on the teapot checking its temperature. All the mothers in our street were known to each other as 'Only Me' and as 'Auntie somebody' to us children. They popped in and out of each other's houses as though they were one big family, no secrets nor barriers. The war had formed these strong bonds of trust but the post-war peace provided the confidence to fulfil their dreams of raising a family, bringing thousands of newly-born children into the world, a generation known as the baby-boomers. My sister and I were part of that boom and we have witnessed the greatest social, cultural and technological changes that the world has seen.

I was born in 1947, just two years after the war. Sixty years on from my earliest memories, I can reflect on the days of my Somerset childhood and marvel at the changes. Imagine how the youngsters of today would cope if we took away their mobile phones, their MP3 players, their PCs and that holy of holies – their television! They'd be mortified but we knew no better.

We had no electricity, so no fridge nor freezer, no washing machine, no bathroom, no hot water on tap, no indoor toilet and no switch-on lights. But we were rich in other ways, members of a closely-bonded community. We could ride our bikes on the main A39 and not worry about cars or lorries. Our food was fresh and locally-grown, and bodily we were allowed, nay even encouraged, to catch every available ailment to ensure we built up our immunities. 'You've got to eat more than one peck of dirt before you die' were my mother's words of wisdom. And peanut allergies didn't exist!

We wore short grey trousers and lived in fear of the local bobby who could give us a smack around the back of the head in the full knowledge that if we told our parents, we'd get another smack from them because we must have been doing something wrong. We respected our teachers, sat at the table for our meals and stood around the piano as our mother played the popular songs of the day. Every mother that lived in our street was called Auntie but their husbands were always 'Mister'. We made our own entertainment and we wasted nothing. We had food rationing and National Service. Our milk was delivered by horse and cart. We wore knitted balaclava helmets, knitted gloves and even (disastrously, usually) knitted swimming costumes. When we played games, it was generally 'war' or British Bulldog. Our playgrounds were the cattle market, the railway track, the pits and the docks. We ate food that few people would see on a plate these days – elvers from the river, tripe, chitterlings and 'bread and scrape'. We wouldn't have been seen dead in trousers with large holes in the knees, unlike the modern vogue where 'designer rips' are a feature. Instead, we all donned short trousers which ended just above the knee – hence grazed knees coated in purple iodine but perfect trousers; well, almost perfect. We used them until we wore through the seat of the pants and even then they weren't thrown away but put aside to earn a few pence from the rag man when he called. Nothing was wasted; on rare occasions unusable food went into the 'pig bins'. Even the language was different. Those were the days when being gay was being happy, when a website was a spider's home and a Big Mac was an extra large raincoat.

Some called them the 'good old days' and they were. We were poor but happy, perhaps just because we were young but I feel it was more than that. In those post-war years of austerity and food rationing, we appreciated the little we had and we learnt to make the best of it with a smile. Oh, happy days!

Roger Evans

In the Beginning

I arrived eighteen months after my sister Pat, in September 1947, just ahead of the National Health Service. It was the time when all medical care had to be paid for. There was very little money in the family, so an ambulance was out of the question, as was the use of a neighbour's car – none of our neighbours possessed one. My parents lived on one side of the River Parrett in Bridgwater and the Mary Stanley Nursing Home was on the other. When my mother recognised the signs of my imminent arrival, she banged on the wall which joined our home to our neighbour's, Violet Morris, and together they began the walk to the nursing home.

My mother and Aunty Vi, as I always knew her, had become close friends when their menfolk were away fighting in the war. In common with all the neighbours in that small avenue of terraced houses, the bonds between them had deepened, sharing the joys and the pains, and their rations. If my mother made a pot of tea (tea being one of the rationed items), she would tap on the wall and Aunty Vi would know that there was a pot brewing. It was natural then that my mother should tap on the wall when her confinement approached.

The shortest route to the nursing home was along the railway spur-line which led to the nearby docks and which crossed the river over Black Bridge, a telescopic railway bridge which could be rolled back when shipping needed to pass up the river. An unofficial but well-used footbridge was attached to one side and consisted of planks spaced apart to reveal the rushing waters through the

With my parents and Bob, the terrier.

gaps. My mother would never use it in normal circumstances, preferring to take the longer route over the town's only road bridge across the river, but when needs must! She nervously completed the crossing and finished the short distance to the nursing home, where I duly arrived.

After my birth, my mother was returned to her bed in the open ward where, sometime later, a smiling nurse entered and presented my mother with the newly-born baby. She took the child in her arms and admired the pretty little face; the process of bonding had begun. Minutes later another nurse, clearly in a state of panic, hurried into the room demanding, 'Who's got baby Williams?' They had given my mother the wrong baby. She always claimed that she instinctively knew the first child was not hers, it was too good-looking! In later years, when she felt the need to chastise me, she would always declare, 'I swear they gave me the wrong baby!'

The Avenue

My early years were spent in Branksome Avenue, a quiet cul-de-sac with just sixteen houses formed in two terraces facing each other across the short length of car-free roadway. Although the avenue ran directly off the main A39 road from Bridgwater to Bath, there was virtually no traffic. Unlike today, very few people had the need for a car; everybody cycled. The nearby Cellophane factory employed 3,500 people and almost all of them rode bikes. At the end of the working day, hundreds of cyclists would go past the top of our avenue on their way home, perhaps as many as a thousand in their mass homeward migration.

It was a close community, with total trust between the neighbouring families. There were no locked doors and burglaries were rarely heard of. Perhaps we had nothing worth stealing and many of the homes still had bare floorboards even when we moved out in 1957. I imagine the only valuable item in our house was the upright piano; not exactly the ideal target for an opportunist thief. If you wanted to visit someone else in the street, you didn't knock and wait, you simply opened the door, shouted, 'Cooee – it's only me' and went on in. We locked our doors at night but it was a bit pointless because everybody in our street kept the key dangling on a piece of string just inside the letter box.

Although the bond between families was usually strong, it was less so in some cases. I remember my mother and Auntie Vi having a go at another neighbour who always felt hard done by, but with no real cause compared to the fortunes of others. In March 1941, my mother had been living in the centre of Plymouth. After two nights of German bombing, only two houses were left standing. She had spent the nights in air raid shelters listening to the destruction all around her. Five months later, she received the telegram informing her that her husband, a Royal Marine Commando, had been killed; his ship torpedoed by a German submarine. The following year, she met and married my father and moved to Somerset. Moving into her Bridgwater home, she asked the inevitable question, 'How bad has the bombing been here?' The neighbour, who always felt hard done by, told her that it had been terrible: 'You've never seen anything like it! We've had a dreadful time.' My mother was soon to discover that Bridgwater had only received a few bombs and learned to take the neighbour's opinion with a pinch of salt. The same lady also complained bitterly when her husband, who was in the Home Guard and so never saw service overseas, was sent away on a two-week training course: 'How am I going to manage when he's away?' My mother and Auntie Vi soon pointed out their menfolk had been away for years at a time, not just weeks, busy fighting the enemy in Europe, Africa or the Far East, so 'stop complaining!'

People who lived in Bridgwater, worked in Bridgwater. If a change of job took the breadwinner to Taunton or elsewhere, then the whole family moved to where the work was. Commuting was neither affordable nor practical. In the absence of cars, the weekly shop was carried home from the local stores. Just around the corner we had Hole and Allen, the grocer's, and there was a butcher, Betty's, the baker, and Mr Irish, the fishmonger, all within a short distance; and there were no such places as supermarkets.

We lived at number 1, an end-of-terrace house next door to Jewell's, the garage-cum-blacksmith's on the corner of the avenue. It was mainly used for the repair and maintenance of tractors. Just a few years before my arrival, it also provided work for Italian prisoners-of-war. My mother, who felt sorry for these unfortunates, would pass cups of tea to them over the fence. Such behaviour could have been considered to be fraternising with the enemy but she always defended her actions, explaining that she hoped her husband, my father, would receive the same kindness if he was ever held as a prisoner-of-war.

As a home, the house lacked the basic facilities. There was no electricity and no bathroom. Downstairs there were three rooms. The front parlour, which was only used on Sundays, was the only room with carpet. On the mantelpiece was a large black-marble clock with pillars either side. Having no electricity at the time, it was a wind-up clock with a slow tick-tock so loud that even with all the doors closed, lying in bed upstairs, it could still be heard. The living room had its coal fire in the corner and was the heart of the home. At the back of the house was the kitchen/scullery.

Upstairs were the three bedrooms plus an attic room. Being an end-of-terrace house, the attic room had a conventional window in the gable end. It was here that my Uncle Roy once 'secretly' stayed. The background to that visit remains a mystery to this day and is a secret my mother took to the grave. She had two younger brothers. The elder was Harold with whom she had a close bond right through their lives. The younger was the mysterious Roy – he who stayed in the attic. I remember being told that we must never mention his presence. A simple explanation could be that, as tenants in a privately-owned house, perhaps we weren't allowed visitors; but it felt more sinister than that and in subsequent conversations with my mother and Harold's widow, the reaction was always the same – 'You are not to speak about him!'

Our home had neither insulation nor double glazing. In the winter, cold winds blew through the letter box and around the ill-fitting doors and window frames. The fireplace was too small for the size of the house, only able to heat the living room, leaving the upstairs perishingly cold. When the temperature dropped outside, we could see our breath as we climbed into bed and we kept our socks on. By morning, ice had formed on the insides of the bedroom windows and, leaning over the side of the bed, I could watch the camel-brown linoleum gently lift from the floorboards as the cold wind billowed beneath it.

Nonetheless, there were others worse off than us. Some lived in the slums of West Street, Clare Street and Market Street where overcrowding

Slum demolition in Clare Street, 1954, ending decades of overcrowding.

9

and poor sanitation had been the source of cholera and dysentery. Through the 1950s, these were demolished and replaced with modern housing.

We had a small back garden where the soil was blackened from years of receiving coal and wood ash from the fireplace. A ramshackle corrugated-iron shed was our storehouse for coal and logs. We also used peat logs which were cheap but gave very little heat. We had an axe and a chopping block on which our father would split logs. My chore was to split the kindling wood – the junior version.

Hen parties and outdoor toilets

Some of our neighbours still had their wartime chicken houses at the bottom of the garden. Most of them were made from recycled materials such as orange crates and tea boxes. Many a chicken house displayed 'Produce of Kenya' on its walls. Aunty Vi next door had one of these. They no longer kept chickens but the hut made a good play house. We had a 'penny jelly' club where my sister and I, along with the neighbouring children, paid a penny a week into a kitty. When there were sufficient funds, we bought jellies and threw a party in the chicken hut.

We had no indoor toilet. It is hard to understand now that there was a time when it was anathema to even consider the thought of 'doing one's toilet' in the same building where you slept and ate your food; how unhygienic! So we had to make do with the outdoor toilet which wasn't so bad except in rough weather and when it was dark. With no electricity, we would light our way to the toilet with a candle in a jam jar, a length of string providing the carrying handle. We lived in fear of the wind blowing out the flickering flame before we even got there and for that reason always walked close to the house wall, along which you could grope your way if need be. Even having safely arrived and closed the door, the ordeal wasn't over. There was no shelf in the toilet, so the candle 'lantern' was placed on the floor just inches from the toilet door which had a three-inch gap at the bottom through which the wind whistled around your ankles, frequently causing the candle to gutter in the draught. Sheets of old newspapers cut into squares and threaded on a string provided the toilet paper and spiders lurked in every nook and cranny. It was no wonder that we kept a chamberpot under our beds.

Tacked onto the back of the house was a single-storey scullery which served as both the kitchen and laundry room. At the end was a large walk-in pantry with a cold slab, the closest thing we had to a fridge. It was here in the scullery that Monday was washday, heralding the start of the weekly rhythm of life.

2

The Rhythm of Life

Monday – washday

Life had a rhythm. First there were the seasons and within each season there was the rhythm of the week. It began with Monday, washday. We had no washing machine or tumble drier but we did have a copper boiler, an upright cylinder with a gas ring below. Cold water was carried by the bucket from the scullery tap to the boiler. The gas ring was lit to bring the water to the boil; soap and bleach being added. Sheets and pillows went in first and were pounded with a wooden pole. Aerated soap bubbles rose until the boiler conceded defeat and allowed the white foam to froth over the top like a badly poured pint of Guinness, spilling onto the stone floor.

The brilliant white sheets were lifted out using wooden tongs, like giant sugar spoons, to be dropped, gushing with scalding hot water, into the galvanised bath in which we washed ourselves at the end of the week. Then they were lifted onto a draining board at the side of a large stone sink to be rinsed under the cold tap, mother's arms now red from the heat and the struggle of pounding and lifting the large, wet and heavy sheets. 'Dolly blue' was added when dealing with the 'whites', which helped to make them even whiter. It always struck me as odd that adding blue to the wash would do this but apparently it masks the yellow stains which would otherwise be more obvious. Inevitably there was a good deal of water over the stone floor. Hence between the boiler and the sink, mother would stand proud on a duck-board, keeping at least her feet dry.

Once rinsed, the sheets went back into the bath, which was dragged into the back yard where a rubber-coated mangle waited to receive the first of the week's laundry, damp sheets emerging from one side whilst water wrung from them gushed from the other, running off over the backyard concrete. The sheets were then straightened, doubled and hung over the washing line using 'gypsy' pegs which our mother took from her kangaroo-pouched apron. On wet days, the washing hung in the scullery, or was draped over clothes horses. It was hard work and the weekly wash filled the whole day, at the end of which our mother was too tired to cook a serious meal. Hence Monday was often bubble and squeak with an egg on top, the previous day's Sunday roast having been produced with an excess of potato and cabbage which were then mixed together and fried in a pan with minimal preparation required.

Tuesday had little going for it other than that it was, and remains, the day that the local paper, the *Bridgwater Mercury*, was published.

Market day – the busiest day of the week

Wednesday was always busy, being market day and, for us, the market was just around the corner. It sadly closed many years ago, now replaced by a giant market close to the motorway junction. Life has moved on since those post-war years and even the livestock looks different. The commonest pigs at the market then were Wessex Saddlebacks, which together with the Essex version accounted for half the pigs in the country. They are now considered a rare breed, replaced by the slimmer pink Landrace which carries both less fat and less flavour.

At the market, you could buy fresh chicken and rabbit. Remember that we had no fridges! It couldn't have been any fresher – meat could be kept indefinitely if it was still alive. However, if you preferred it dead, then the stallholder would oblige.

Miss Aish, an elderly lady, was the auctioneer at the market. She once held a national claim to fame as the last trader in the UK to convert to decimal coinage. Some fifteen years after the introduction of decimalisation, she would confuse the youngsters as she invited bids: 'Right, who'll start me off with thrupence. Thank you, sir. Do I see a tanner? Ninepence anyone? Thank you. A shilling, one and six, two bob, half a crown, three shillings. Any advance on three bob? Three shillings for the last time. Sold.' It was like a foreign language and she was actually threatened with court action for failing to convert. She was Britain's last bastion of pounds, shillings and pence.

We always knew when it was market day, even before we got out of bed. Although most cattle arrived by lorry, you could hear the sheep and cattle being herded along the road. Even into the late 1950s, sheep and cattle were still brought down on foot from hill villages such as Broomfield. I remember a group of bullocks destined for the fat stock market being driven along the Bath road. One decided to lie down and take a rest. The herdsman grabbed it by the ear and shouted very loudly into it. The bullock looked at the man with disgust, got to its feet and finished the final hundred yards to the market.

Day-old chicks could be purchased and were gently lifted out from beneath a broody hen and handed over in a brown paper bag, just like

The fat stock show at Bridgwater market, 1959.

buying a bag of loose sweets. Many homes, even in the towns, had a fowl house in the back garden. It made sense to keep your own chickens during the years of wartime rationing and the practice continued well into peace-time.

If a brown paper bag seems an unusual way to get livestock home, a Bentley is even stranger. He was clearly a city gent; you could tell by his dress and his 'posh' voice. Apparently he had bought an old farmhouse on the Quantock Hills where he was going to live the country life. He arrived at Bridgwater market set on purchasing a young calf. The sale was agreed at the auction and then came the problem of getting it home. He had no trailer. He had assumed that you could put it in the back of the car and it would behave itself like a well-trained dog. The locals couldn't believe what they were witnessing and in fairness did their best to advise him against the action. But he knew best! And so three of them managed to get the young calf into the back seat of the Bentley where it promptly relieved itself!

Early closing day

Imagine realising that you had run out of milk or bread and it was five minutes past one o'clock on a Thursday afternoon. Your only hope was to borrow from a neighbour. The shops were all shut. Thursday was early closing day. It seems unbelievable today when we have grown accustomed to late-night shopping and supermarkets open seven days a week with their rows of busy tills.

There were other occasions when the shops would close, perhaps for a celebration, such as the Coronation, but more commonly for a funeral. It is unlikely today that a shop would close for such a situation, even if it was for one of its own staff, but in the 1950s shops closed simply because a funeral would be passing by. Even when someone was dying, the community showed how much it cared. In the Somerset villages, straw or sawdust would be laid in the road to reduce the noise of passing horses and wagons, and dogs given a bone to chew to stop them barking.

Communities were closer in those post-war days and sharing grief was a feature of the culture. I remember the telegram boys on their push bikes, who would make their deliveries of little brown envelopes. Telegrams were invariably bad news and the neighbours had grown accustomed to their arrival in the war years with short, blunt messages such as 'Regret to inform you…killed in action' or '…missing presumed dead'. After my mother died, I discovered one that she had received early in the war informing her of her first husband's death. 'Regret to inform you…' was the only hint of compassion. The neighbours, on such occasions, having been there so many times before, would leave it for five or ten minutes before gathering around the recipient to give their moral support.

Pay day

Friday was pay day. Perhaps that explains why the shops closed early on Thursdays. Everyone was paid weekly and everyone was paid in cash; no cheque books; few bank accounts. I remember opening my first savings account as a child at the post office around the corner. It was run by Mr Nation and I was probably seven or eight years old. The interest rate was sixpence in the pound (2.5%) and had been for years. Being a newly-opened post office, my account number was rather low: *Bath Road, Bridgwater account number 7*! Compare that to a six digit sort code followed by an eight digit account number. Everything in my little savings book was handwritten and elsewhere the Post Office accounts department would likewise have a handwritten ledger reflecting the value of my savings. No computers in those days.

Being pay day, mother would send me down the road to see Bert Hole at Hole and Allen to pick up our weekly grocery shopping. I would already have gone down two or three days before with a list of what we needed and Mr Hole would have ordered just what was required. That was how it worked before pre-packaged goods and chill cabinets arrived. I also took our ration books if meat or sugar products were involved. Neighbours often traded their ration coupons. Perhaps if a birthday was coming up and extra sugar was needed for a cake, then a neighbour would lend or swap a coupon, but they had to be used up quickly because they were dated. You couldn't save up your coupons; they had to be used in the nominated week or lost.

My mother had a rather unusual extra source for her sugar ration. We had a tramp that would visit us every now and then, because he knew that my mother would feed him. He was a well-spoken man and never expected something for nothing, so mother would give him a carpet to beat, a basket of logs to split or some similar chore, but he was never allowed in the house. By the time his chore was complete, mother would have prepared his meal which he ate on the doorstep. He never used sugar and when rationing was introduced, he remembered mother's kindness and from then on gave her his sugar ration.

Items like loaves of bread were always available, if you got to the shop early enough in the day, and it was a great treat to be asked by one of my

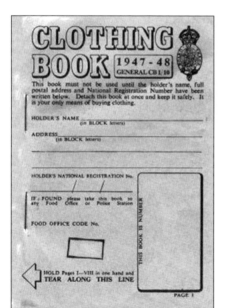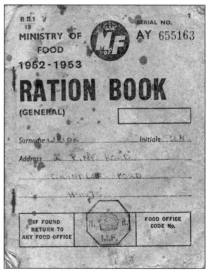

Post-war ration books for clothing and food. (Courtesy of Warwick Wride)

many 'aunties' to fetch them a loaf, since this was always rewarded with 'and a penny for yourself'. This could buy a liquorice strip, a gobstopper or perhaps a bag of aniseed balls, all of which were held in screw top jars behind the counter.

Sometimes I had to go further afield to the Co-op where, having completed the purchase, the lady behind the counter would ask, 'Your divi number?' '19801,' I would reply and the amount we spent would be entered against my mother's Co-op membership number. That would later be used to determine what my mother's share of the company's profits was at the end of the year. It was an early form of loyalty card and 60 years on I can still remember the number, it was so engrained.

The Co-op held a real fascination because of the way they handled money. They were the closest thing we had to a supermarket of today – with cashiers. There were no tills containing cash downstairs. Instead the lady who served you would write down a list of all the items you purchased and then would take your cash and place it in a screw-top tin, about the size of a baked bean tin. The cash tin was placed into a metal pipework system which used vacuum to suck it upstairs where the total amount was checked and the appropriate change put in the tin to be blasted back to the lady serving you. Every few feet along the pipework was a glass window allowing you to follow the container speeding its way to the upstairs cashiers. It was a system the Co-op had introduced right across the country and fascinated many a young child.

The working community trusted the Co-op. It was non-profit-making and promised good value for money. During the war years, fashion became an unnecessary luxury and 'Utility' goods were introduced. This covered everything from clothing to furniture. The result was that everybody tended to dress the same and had the same style of furniture – but it didn't matter because there was a war on. Once the war was over, fashion began to creep back in. You could still buy Utility goods but most people preferred to be seen to be wearing better. Utility goods carried the Utility label and hence were less expensive. However, one clever lady at the Co-op found that she could supplement her income by cutting the Utility labels off pairs of gloves and selling them at a higher price, pocketing the difference for herself. Needless to say she was given her cards once her scheme was discovered.

Saturday matinee and Bridgwater Manchets

Saturday was mother's most serious cleaning day. My sister and I would disappear for the morning blessed with 7d each. That covered the 1d return bus fare to the Odeon cinema and the 6d entry to the morning matinee children's performance. On the bus and at the cinema, we had the theoretical choice of upstairs or downstairs. On the bus it was an easy choice, upstairs – front seats, if available and they usually were. The top deck was the reserve of smokers, smoking being banned on the lower deck. Although they weren't banned from the front of the bus, smokers generally sat at the back out of courtesy to the other travellers. This always struck me as odd. I guess the theory was that if the bus was moving forward, the smoke would drift to the back. Now that was probably true in the days of open-top, horse-drawn carriages but not true of a covered-top double-decker bus. It fact, what it meant was that since access to the top deck was at the rear of the bus, the non-smokers still had to walk through the smoke. Buses in those days did not have closing doors to stop people getting on or off, nor did passengers go past the driver on the way in. The rear of the bus was open and you could jump on and off whilst it was still moving. Only the driver's cab was closed off and each bus carried a conductor who would collect the money and distribute the tickets.

At the cinema, better-off families paid the 9d for their children to use the balcony where the customers were better behaved. Downstairs was a different matter with the small kids towards the front and the big boys at the back. From there they would use rubber bands to fire folded-paper pellets at the back of the heads of the smaller fry. These were the same boys that pushed their way to the front of the queue when we were waiting to go in. No one viewed it as bullying – it was just part of growing up, the natural order of things.

Watching the films, we sat on the red-velvety seats ensuring our hands never went beneath where countless lumps of chewing gum lurked ready to attach themselves to the first inquisitive fingertip. As we waited for the films to start, someone would stamp their feet which was the signal for us all to join in. Shouted commands from the usherettes, demanding we behave, were ignored but once the net curtain was opened to reveal the silver screen, the auditorium fell silent – briefly. The noise levels were unbelievable during the films when we would boo the villains, cheer the heroes and shout 'Behind you' as if the characters could hear us.

There was always a cartoon, a western and a science fiction movie. The Lone Ranger, Roy Rogers and the Cisco Kid were all favourite western characters where the good guys wore white whilst the bad guys wore black and were normally unshaven. The exception was Zorro, the hero, who was always dressed in black. These films, along with the Buck Rogers and Dan Dare science fiction movies, were serials where, at the end of each

17

weekly episode, the hero would be left in some perilous situation making it essential to return the following week to see whether or not he survived. As an example, the Lone Ranger would be galloping towards the edge of a cliff and his horse would go right over the edge. The film would stop with the horse and rider in mid-air, doomed to plummet to a fatal end as a voice declared: 'Will the Lone Ranger finally fall to his death? Don't miss next week's exciting episode!' The following week the film would pick up the story from the same point – well, almost. Just before the horse reached the cliff edge, the Lone Ranger would pull him up just in time and you would be left wondering if your memory had played tricks with you. Equally miraculous was the ability of the cowboys to fire scores of shots from their six-shooters with never the need to reload!

Once the Saturday matinee was over, we'd catch the bus home where we would find our mother cleaning the brass door knocker. As soon as we left for the cinema, she started cleaning the house, from top to bottom and from the back to the front. The front door knocker was the last item of her morning session. Shortly after, our father would arrive home having finished his shift at the post office and bringing with him a paper bag of Bridgwater Manchets, a jam-filled pastry delicacy unique to Bridgwater.

The town was blessed with two other cinemas, the Rex (known as the Flea Pit or the Bug House) and the Palace. There had been even more at one time, some of which had been introduced to entertain the American troops who were stationed nearby, but as television increased its influence, so the number of cinemas declined to the present solitary one. The Rex had a somewhat seedy reputation. Not only was it called the flea pit for obvious reasons, but it was also noted for the 'immoral' behaviour of those who chose the back row. The Rex still had gas lights around the walls although the projection was powered by electricity. One trick played by the older lads was to blow hard on the gas lights to break the fragile mantle, the part which glowed to produce a white light. The attendants were unable to repair these while the film was running and hence the back-rowers could do as they pleased, undetected in total darkness.

Short back and sides

Once a fortnight, my father and I would go to Mr Verncombe's, the local barber on the Bristol road. There, on a Saturday afternoon, the local men would gather on the long horse-hair padded wooden benches as they awaited their turn to take the chair. As a young boy, I was required to sit on a wooden plank placed across the arms of the barber's chair and remain perfectly still while he administered the regulation short back and sides. There was only one hairstyle known to our barber and it reflected the style used when men did their National Service. Nonetheless, it was better than the alternative which was known as a basin-cut. In the school playground, you would be the laughing stock with everyone knowing that your parents couldn't afford for you to go to the barber's. Instead it was your mother who cut your hair, getting a straight edge to the fringe by placing a pudding basin on your head.

Waiting in the barber's was tedious for a young child and it was never possible to predict how long you would need to wait. Some men extended their stay by having a 'singe', whereby Mr Verncombe would run a comb through the hair with one hand whilst holding a lighted taper in the other with which he would singe the hair ends. A short back and sides didn't take too long but many of the men would also require a shave and that took ages.

There was a ritual to the proceedings. Mr Verncombe would apply a generous layer of white foaming lather to the customer's neck and cheeks. This he brewed up in a shaving mug with boiling water, working it in vigorously with his shaving brush. The customer was left to 'soften up' whilst he sharpened his cut-throat razor. He would take one end of a leather strop, the other end still attached to the chair. Holding this stretched out before him, he stroked the razor back and forth, getting a fine edge which he tested by running his thumb along the blade. He would then slice off a strip of paper which was placed on the customer's shoulder before he applied the razor to the customer's chin. With each stroke of the razor, he would wipe the surplus lather onto the paper. He was a master of his craft, rarely nicking the flesh and glowing with satisfaction as he lifted the customer's nose tip to shave off the final and most difficult bit just beneath the nostrils and across the top lip. I used to wonder if these men went in every day for a shave because my father shaved daily at home, but later realised that these were the ones who shaved once a week and then on Saturday because it was their night out.

On the wall in front of the barber's chair was a pair of mirrors, one to either side and angled slightly inwards. On completing a haircut, Mr Verncombe would hold another mirror around the back of your head and ask, 'Is that OK, young man?' For the men, it was a different question: 'Anything for the weekend, sir?' Contraceptives were kept out of sight and it was either at the barber's or in the pubs that they were purchased. A short little man, locally known as Noah, used to visit the town pubs wearing a long brown raincoat which, having identified his target, he would open up like a phantom-flasher to reveal his range of contraceptive brands adorning the lining of his coat. The question was the same, 'Anything for the weekend, sir?'.

Saturday night and the once-a-week bath

If Saturday began with the cinema, it ended with the family bath night. Because we had no running hot water and no bathroom, having a bath was a long-winded affair. Our mother began by filling the copper boiler with water, lighting the gas ring beneath and bringing the water nearly to the boil. In our back yard, a galvanised tin bath hung on a nail on the outside wall. Once a week it was brought indoors, part filled with cold water and then brought up to comfortably hot with water bailed out from the boiler using our largest saucepans. Because I was the youngest, I went in first and was scrubbed, then my sister, then mother and finally father, by which time the water was tepid and already had a layer of scum from the previous three occupants who hadn't had a bath for at least a week. Finally, when all were finished, my father and I dragged the bath of water out into the back yard where it was tipped out and I would then brush down the yard with a hard-bristled brush.

While I was still at infant school, the family went to visit Uncle Matthias in the Taff Valley, in a mining village near Treforest. We were there in the living room just before tea-time and heard the sound of miners walking up the valley road between the long rows of terraced miners' cottages. Uncle Matthias walked through the front door, as black as the ace of spades. In front of the fireplace, the tin bath of hot water was already waiting for him. My mother and sister disappeared into the kitchen, whilst my father and I stayed to chat with Uncle Matthias. He stripped off all his clothing to expose the limited white parts of his body and slowly stepped into the bath. Up and down that valley, the same process was being repeated. As he washed his face, arms and legs, my aunty washed his hair and scrubbed his back. It was a culture shock to me. I had no idea that a grown man would be naked before my very eyes, let alone with my mother and sister in the house.

When I was ten years old, we moved out of the Branksome Avenue terrace and into a brand new council house on the Sydenham Estate. It was quite exciting not just because we had open countryside at the bottom of the garden, but because we had a bathroom and a hot-water tank with an immersion heater. The bath had both hot and cold taps and a plug! No more dragging the bathwater into the back yard. For the first few weeks, we had a bath every night!

Sunday – not much of a day of rest

Our mother was a Methodist which meant we went every Sunday morning to the Monmouth Street Methodist church, one of two Wesleyan chapels in Bridgwater. Occasionally, our mother would play the manually-pumped wind organ. Sunday afternoons was Sunday school (where our mother was a teacher) and then home for tea. Quite often, while we were eating our sandwiches and cake (which was a Sunday treat), we would hear the Salvation Army band playing on the corner of the avenue. They were the one religious group which my father was prepared to support and his prejudice was based on his wartime experiences. He argued that when he came out of the desert after several weeks of heavy action, the Salvation Army were the only religious group present, and they were waiting with fresh socks, soup and soap, all of which were desperately needed.

Sunday evening normally saw us back in church again. It was a lot of religion to take on board at such a young age but there were fringe benefits which came with Sunday school. Every member of the Sunday school had a record card which was stamped with a gold star for each attendance. Anyone attending at least ten times in a year qualified for the annual outing to the seaside at Burnham-on-Sea. This involved a ten-mile train ride on the old Somerset and Dorset Railway. We all took a packed lunch and would hit the beach as soon as we arrived.

Some lads attended more than one church in order to reap the maximum benefit. Some years ago, I was reflecting on those trips and

With my sister Pat on a day-trip to the seaside.

21

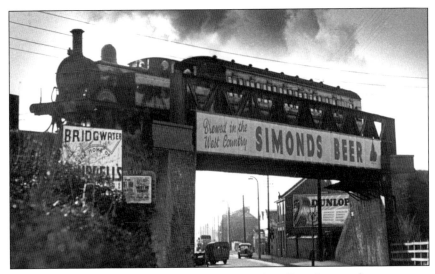

The S & D (Somerset and Dorset) train returns from Burnham-on-Sea.

discussing them with an old friend of my late father's, Don Templeman. Don was into his nineties and told me how he too had gone to the Monmouth Street Methodist just for the summer outing. He produced an old attendance card to convince me but I noticed that it was actually from the Baptist chapel. 'Yes,' explained Don, 'I went to the Monmouth Street Methodist, King Street Methodist, Baptist and Mariners' chapels. I went to Burnham four times a year. We'd go off in the back of a farm cart. Of course, the driver wasn't supposed to take so many children so we all had to lie down beneath the canvas until we got outside of the town and then we could sit up and enjoy the view.'

Our family also attended the Mariners' chapel for a while. It came about when the Methodist church decided to run bingo as a fundraiser. Mother, being staunch Methodist, was totally against drinking and gambling. It was one step too far. Meanwhile, as we worshipped at the Methodist chapel, father worshipped at the Cross Rifles. It was a wonderful childhood with contrasting parental influences. Our mother had been raised in the Salvation Army, later turning Methodist, and set high moral standards. Our father, by contrast, was a regular social drinker who had been a boxer and wrestler travelling on the fairgrounds. He was street-wise and encouraged an adventurous spirit. Whilst our mother would often start a conversation with 'Bill, you've got to talk to that boy!', father finished it with, 'Leave the boy alone. He's got to learn.'

3

What, No Television?

Listen with Mother

It was difficult to contemplate the prospect of television when we didn't even have electricity and, as young children, we were totally unaware of its existence. Although television had been around since the 1930s, it was strictly the reserve of the wealthy. We did, however, have a piano and eventually a radio when electricity was finally installed on the ground floor of our home. The benefit of radio was that we could listen as a family whilst sitting around the fire and still having a conversation. The family and the fireplace were the focus. With TV, it's the box which becomes the focus and the family unit which loses out. We listened to such programmes as *Listen with Mother, Around the Horne* and *The Goons*.

As an alternative, mother played the piano, using sheet music stored in the box seat of her piano stool. She was a good pianist and often played at the local church, especially for the Sunday school. As youngsters we joined in the musical experience using a comb and toilet paper. Toilet paper in the Fifties was much stiffer than the 'soft as a baby's face' version that you get today. It could be folded over a comb, held against the lips and then, by humming against the paper, a Kazoo-like sound could be created and tunes played to support mother's piano performance. We were also great players of board games (Ludo, Snakes and Ladders) and cards (Snap and Happy Families when we were very young, and then Newmarket and Rummy), our mother passing on the knowledge of games she had learnt in turn from her mother.

Story telling

The fireplace was the heart of the family home. During winter months, the first duty of the morning was to rake out the previous day's ashes and 'lay the fire'. Scrunched up newspaper was lain beneath a layer of kindling wood, and then logs or coals on top of that. Having lit the paper balls, a sheet of newspaper would be held across the small fireplace to 'draw the flames'. Sometimes it took longer than others and it was not unusual, having looked the other way momentarily, to turn back and see the drawing-paper on fire.

Our mother was a great one for telling stories and many a winter's evening we sat around the fire and listened to tales of her childhood or the war years. She told how, as a young girl, she had very long hair, which was much sought after by wig makers. My grandmother had been asked to sell my mother's long tresses but had refused. As a result, my mother answered a knock at the door one day to find the same man standing on the doorstep. Before she knew what was happening he had grabbed the hair on one side of her head, hacked it off and escaped. My horrified grandmother was faced with cutting the hair from the other side to tidy up the mess.

Some of her stories were of a sadder nature. She talked of her mother's brother, Uncle Albert, who went to war in 1915. She had clear memories of watching her mother give Albert a Cornish pasty which he put in his pocket. My mother at three years old was concerned that the pasty would get damaged in his pocket, unaware of the real dangers of war. Albert was one of those who never returned. She loved telling these family tales and it filled a gap which is now taken over by the television. I'm convinced our lives were the richer for our relative poverty.

TV and the thunderbolt

Our first televisual experience came in June 1953. It was the day of the Coronation of Queen Elizabeth ll. A friend of our father, another postman called Aubrey Ryder, had a television set, the first we ever saw. We were invited to join him in his council house on the Sydenham Estate. The front room was packed to the rafters with about 50 friends and family. A dozen or more children sat immediately in front of the television with their knees tucked up so as to take as little floor space as possible. It was nonetheless an exciting experience for many of those present which convinced them that they too should have their own television, my mother included. Some weeks later, after a visit to Radio Rentals, our own set arrived and each day thence, all the kids in our avenue would arrive in time for *Children's Hour*, which was from 5 to 6 o'clock. There was always a groan when it was switched on because the sound, which came from behind a piece of brown woven cloth about the size of a dinner plate, would come on first with no picture. After a minute or so of hopeful anticipation, the grey and white images would appear on the screen. Once the programme was over, the television would be switched off and we all watched as the picture shrank to a small white gradually-disappearing dot. Like watching a sunset, no one moved until the dot had disappeared.

It was during one of those shared moments that our house was struck by a thunderbolt. Those who saw it from outside described it as a ball of electrical energy which first hit the roof of our house and then ran along the ridge of the terrace, taking down chimney pots before it shot across the grounds of a nearby factory to attack another terrace, finally burning out in the road. Inside we heard the bang as the bolt hit. The lightning had made a direct hit on the aerial and a charge of energy had shot down the cable. Our nearly new, but fortunately rented, television burst into flames.

Of course there was only the one channel, the BBC, and everything was in black and white. *Children's Hour* was followed by the news and then the channel went off the air for a while in order that parents could pack the children off to bed. In theory we were not supposed to know that the TV then came back on but secrets like that can never be kept for long. Consequently, my sister and I would sit on the stairs and take it in turns to peep through a crack in the panelled timber wall which separated the staircase from the living room. The walls were very thin and the sound of the television carried quite well into our bedrooms. One evening, just as we were dropping off to sleep, we heard a terrifying scream from downstairs and were convinced that our father was murdering our mother. Rushing downstairs to the rescue, we found them side by side on the settee, quietly watching the TV. It was our first experience of hearing opera in the house!

Activities

Although television had finally arrived, there was only one hour set aside for children. We still needed to fill our time and burn off energy. Racing trolleys, or soap-box carts as we knew them, were great sport and these were always home-made using two sets of pram wheels (Silver Cross were the best) and a few planks. One long plank provided the chassis. At the back end of this was fixed perhaps an orange or soap box as a seat, beneath which were the rear wheels. At the front end, a short length of plank with wheels attached was fixed across the chassis with a nut, bolt and series of washers so that it could be steered, using a length of rope. Up and down the avenue we would race making the appropriate 'Stirling Moss' noises.

In cold weather, our woollen knitted gloves were never enough to keep out the cold, so we used home-made hand warmers. These were fashioned from old cocoa tins, with removable lids. Holes were punched into each end using a meat skewer and then smouldering rags placed inside to provide half an hour's warmth.

We used to play Ratatat-Ginger, a simple game where you knock on somebody's door and run away before they can emerge and spot you. It was a game which you never played in your own street, but one nearby. Our homes were all terraced houses, with long rows on either side of the street. This provided the opportunity for a more complicated version of Ratatat-Ginger. There was always plenty of black cotton in everybody's houses, used to repair clothes. The trick was to tie one end of a length of cotton to a door knocker and the other end to another immediately across the road. Then you would knock the first door and run. When the person from the first house opened their door, that would pull the length of cotton which would cause the door knocker opposite to be lifted. When the person closed their door, the knocker on the opposite side would sound and that person would answer their door. In theory, it was possible to connect the second door knocker to a third house, next door to the first, and so on, but that all took time and increased the risk of being caught!

Cubs and Boy Scouts provided a weekly diversion and since my mother was an Akela, one of the Scout pack leaders, I was bound to go. I was about seven or eight years old when I joined and each of us was given Lord Baden-Powell's handbook, *Scouting for Boys*. Its origins were in the Boer War and it showed pictures of how to stalk an enemy and how to follow lion spoors. It was all exciting stuff but the reality was that the closest we got to tracking Boer guerrillas was to follow a trail of wooden tapers, and these always went out of the back door of the church hall, around the block and back in the front of the church hall; always the same route! So the main interest was collecting proficiency badges for skills such as fire-lighting or knot tying. The badges were stitched to the sleeve of your cub jersey and the target was to get an armful. Call me boring but I actually found a trip to the library more exciting.

I was always a great reader and Bridgwater was blessed with two good libraries. The first was the Bridgwater Free Library, founded with money from the American steel magnate Andrew Carnegie. This was for the townsfolk of Bridgwater, and then there was the county library for anyone in Somerset. Once a fortnight, I'd visit both, picking up four books from each. Who gets enough time these days to read that many books when there's so much television to watch?

Dressed in my Cub Scout uniform.

During the long summer holidays, we would spend whole days at the town's swimming pool which was an open-air lido, with lawned areas and three separate pools catering for different ability levels. Hundreds of local children benefited from the open-air pool until the council, in its wisdom, decided that what we needed was an indoor pool to provide all-year swimming. So the Lido site was sold off – to a supermarket obviously – and the new pool built, complete with flumes and wave machines. The contractors went bust during its construction and corners were cut to get the work completed. Those cut corners came back to haunt the council and created a never-ending list of maintenance problems. The council, again in its wisdom, decided that a new pool was to be built. So they demolished the indoor pool having sold the site for, yes – you've guessed it – another supermarket. The town now has no swimming pool. But I have allowed myself to wander into the present. It's time to return to the past.

27

All the fun of the fair

Autumn heralded a series of popular events starting with the fair and ending with Christmas. The last Wednesday in September, St Matthew's Day, has provided the first day of Bridgwater Fair for hundreds of years. Originally a one-day hiring fair, it is now a four-day funfair and probably the biggest in the West of England. On the Wednesday morning, there were the sheep and pony sales, the latter attracting a large number of gypsies, as well as Quantock Hill farmers. The Quantock commoners are allowed to graze their ponies on the common land on the Quantock Hills

The Meteor and 'Coles Famous Gondolas' at Bridgwater Fair.

28

and just before Bridgwater Fair, they would organise a massive round-up of the ponies, a number of which were sold at the fair. These were unbroken, wild ponies but also at the fair were the well-mannered gypsy ponies. To demonstrate how manageable they were, young gypsy boys would trot them up and down, riding them bare-back. Once a price was agreed, the traditional way to seal the deal was for the seller and the buyer each to spit on the palm of their own hand before slapping palms with the other person.

Once the sales were over, it was the huge funfair which took priority for the full four days. In my youth, there were two beer tents, plus the Horse and Jockey, a pub on the very edge of the fairground. These were clustered together at one end of the Fairfield which inevitably meant that this was where any punch-ups took place. It was here that I spent most of my time at the fair. My father had once been a traveller on the fairgrounds as a boxer and wrestler. He had learned to box in the Navy between the two world wars. Having left the Navy, he travelled the West

The boxing booth at Bridgwater Fair, where my father always finished the season.

Country with the fair during the summer months, visiting Plymouth, Barnstaple, Bideford and other places, but always finishing the season at Bridgwater before the winter retirement, during which time he worked as a postman in Bridgwater. Some well-known names from yesteryear have boxed at Bridgwater Fair, including world champion Freddie Mills and the famous Turpin brothers.

The striptease act and the hoopla stall

Next to the McKeown family's boxing booth was the striptease tent, which usually needed a gimmick such as a knife-throwing act as part of the performance. 'Roll up, roll up, roll up. She's alive and showing on the inside,' the barker would shout. 'Eve without leaves. She wears nothing, absolutely nothing. Step inside, sir. Ladies especially welcome.' Night after night as a six-year-old I listened to him as I worked on the hoopla stall whilst father was in the boxing booth or taking monies on the Jungle Ride.

My role on the hoopla stall was to help whip up a crowd. I would be given a set of three rings which I had to throw over the prizes on the stall. The most popular item was the ten-bob note (50p) which was wrapped around a cylinder about the size of a toilet roll tube. The ring to be

The striptease show, 'Eve without leaves'.

30

thrown was about eight inches across and would easily fit over the cylinder with the note attached. The catch was that the eight-inch ring actually needed to fit over the square wooden block on which the cylinder stood. The block was sized so that the ring would just, and only just, fit over it. The least sideways movement, which was inevitable when throwing the ring onto the stall, would stop the ring fitting over the block.

Before the stallholder gave me the rings, and ensuring no one saw him do it, he would fit a ring over the block on which stood a two-pound jar of sweets, almost as big as myself. My job was to wait for the stall holder to go around to the other side of the stall and then throw my three rings. Once I had thrown the third one, I would shout 'Mister! Mister! I've won, I've won, I've got the sweets!' He would then come around to check and, lo and behold, there was a ring perfectly sitting around the wooden block. 'And another lucky winner,' he would shout. 'Come on, folks. Everyone's a winner. Well done, Sonny Jim. Here's your sweets. Off you go. Give someone else a chance to win.' As the crowd gathered, I'd walk slowly away, beaming from ear to ear, saying, 'Cor, look what I've won!' There's one born every minute, so they say. The crowd would hand over their hard-earned cash and lose it. I'd go and watch the barker at the striptease tent or the boxers on the speedballs until a whistle from the stall signalled my time to return and whip up the next crowd.

In later years, by which time I was in my teens, I was at the fair with 'the gang', a group of about six of us. We managed to sneak into the striptease tent and watch the show. The strippers were dreadful; they looked bored stiff, performed dreadfully and were as skinny as rakes. Whilst the performance was disappointing from one aspect, it was hilarious from another. It was the banter and the wisecracks from the crowd which provided the entertainment. 'I've seen more meat on a butcher's apron!' shouted one of our gang, closely followed by another with, 'Yeh, more fat on a cold chip!'

The beer tent and the gypsies

Next to the striptease show was the beer tent run by Fred Cavill. This was another source of boxing but of the unofficial kind. It often involved the gypsy community but they always looked after their own. If there was a dispute to be settled, the gypsies would form a circle around the two combatants to let them sort it out between themselves. These brief encounters were normally right outside the entrance to the beer tent. The lady who sold cockles and mussels in dishes of vinegar from a little trestle table was sufficiently experienced to recognise the warning signs, at which point she would pick up her table and disappear inside the tent until the heat had died down. The beer tent was a favourite haunt for the gypsies since in those pre-politically-correct days, almost every pub in town displayed a 'No gypsies served here' notice in the windows. They also declared 'No Irish', being at the time that there was a large influx of Irish labour, particularly for the building of Hinkley Point nuclear power station. Such signs disappeared with the introduction of the Race Relations Act.

The fighting wasn't always on the Fairfield. Sometimes it spilled over into other parts of the town. One year, a courting couple were at the fair and the lad had won a set of kitchen knives. Somewhere during the course of the evening, the girl he was with had gone off with another fellow. The drink was in. On the way home, the aggrieved lad stabbed and killed his adversary. It was just a matter of yards from our front door. The perpetrator was found guilty and sentenced to imprisonment. Not many years earlier this would have brought the death penalty.

West Street, the road leading to the fairground, has always provided a range of stalls which sell almost anything. Before the days of trading standards, much of what was sold was of dubious quality. A stallholder would demonstrate perhaps a glass cutter which would never blunt, but the one you bought from him would work once and then never again. Those rogues have all gone and today it's the more honest traders who come back year after year, but with the disappearance of the rogues, we have also lost some really entertaining and colourful characters.

The largest night-time carnival in the world

October came close on the heels of Bridgwater Fair and brought the carnival concerts, acting as a prelude to the gigantic November carnival procession. Since this event is linked to the Guy Fawkes celebrations, it comes at the time of the bonfires and the fireworks that go with them. My introduction to fireworks was with the simple sparkler, a metal rod fused with iron filings which sparkle as they burn and can be hand-held by a child. We lit these in the fire and then took them outside to whirl them around. When I was about six years old, I tried to relight my sparkler by putting it in the newly installed electric fire with literally shocking results. I remember my father's anger as he had to repair the fuse. In those days of my infancy, it was common practice for exploding fireworks to be thrown into the crowds which thronged the streets. For that reason alone, we wore our oldest clothes, often with the coat inside-out, so that any burns didn't show. We also wore wellington boots to protect our feet against exploding 'rook scarers', used in farming and considerably more lethal than the conventional penny banger. My mother once received one which landed inside her boot and exploded before she could kick her boot off. Her leg went black and blue and she ended up in hospital. As a carnival dressmaker, making costumes for a number of clubs, she deserved better. Being the son of a carnival dressmaker meant that I was sworn to secrecy about the costumes which I saw being made in our home. It also provided the opportunity for an introduction to the world of carnival, a community of which I have been a member throughout my life.

I was about four years old when I took part in my first procession with my sister as 'The Wee Folk from Holland', dressed as a Dutch boy and girl. Aged seven, I was given my first opportunity to take part in the big time, on one of the major floats. My mother was dressmaker to two different clubs, the Hope Inn and Cardiff Arms carnival clubs. The Hope Inn's theme for their 1954 entry was 'At the Races'. Lester Piggott, the jockey sensation of the age, was known as the Boy Wonder. The club

The Hope Inn's At The Races *in 1954 – I am the young jockey, centre-front.*

needed someone about the same size as the diminutive Piggott. As a very small seven year old, I was perfect. My mother did a costume in his racing colours and I was up on one of the big floats for the first time in my life. The float was simple enough in design. It was just a load of plywood cut-out horses about an inch thick and we each had a saddle on which to sit which was about four inches wide. It was most uncomfortable, especially since the procession could take an hour or more.

We took third place at Bridgwater as a singing and dancing feature and moved on to the North Petherton carnival which took place two days later. The committee there, who have always been difficult to deal with, decided that since most of us were sat on horses, we couldn't really be dancing. Tableau entries kept perfectly still as though portraying a picture. We were told that if we were to enter, we would have to take part as a tableau. Aged seven, I had to stay perfectly still for about an hour on a moving float, or cart as they are traditionally called in carnival circles. The good news was that we took first place as a tableau and were allowed to finish the next five carnivals as a feature.

As a young turbaned slave boy with the Cardiff Arms' Eastern Fantasies in 1955.

The following year, I was back in the carnival harness as a slave boy performing with the Cardiff Arms club in their 'Eastern Fantasies' portrayal. Shepton Mallet carnival was memorable for me that year because it was so cold. Dressed in a slave boy's costume (admittedly with a couple of vests beneath), I was perishing cold and shivering, as were the rest of the performers. Dot Bond was one of the members dressed as slave girls and she took pity on me. She had a flask of brandy – to help keep the cold out. She knew that my mother was a Methodist and against alcohol but, nonetheless, she was determined I should be protected from the elements: 'Here you go, love. Have a couple of swigs of that to keep the cold out. But don't tell your mum.' Oh, it was powerful stuff. I didn't particularly like the flavour but the warm glow as it slid down was a wonderful and new sensation. The second swig was just as comforting. Shortly after, as the time to start the procession approached, Val Boley sneaked up to me. She was another of the club's young ladies. She too was concerned for my welfare and provided the same level of comfort – 'But don't tell your mum!' I have no further recollections of that night but I'll put that down to the passing years!

A Somerset Christmas

The November carnivals were followed by Christmas and we still believed in Santa Claus. Our last chore on Christmas Eve was to put out the plate on the front step with a few carrots for the reindeer and a mince pie and glass of milk for Father Christmas. Most families in our street put out a glass of sherry, but our mother was a Methodist! Christmas was a double-edged sword in our house. Mother loved it; so did my sister and I, but my father hated it with a passion. He was a postman! For two weeks we would hardly ever see him as he worked double shifts, arriving home after we'd gone to bed and leaving again before we got up. It was normally later on Christmas Day that we finally got to sit down with him, by which time he was too tired to care.

At Christmas we were allowed into the front room, normally only permitted on Sundays or when special visitors came. We decorated the house with home-made paper chains and a real Christmas tree. Artificial trees had yet to make an appearance. It was also the time of year when chestnuts were in season and these we roasted on the open fire, placing a dozen or so on the coal shovel and letting that rest in the flames until the first chestnut burst open, providing the signal that the rest were ready.

Our Christmas puddings were always home-made and by tradition there was a silver threepenny bit, or latterly a silver sixpenny bit hidden in the pudding. He who found the lucky slice got to keep the sixpence. It seems odd now to reflect back on the coins we had. We had farthings (a quarter penny), halfpennies, pennies, threepenny and sixpenny bits, shillings, florins (two shillings), half crowns (two shillings and sixpence) and ten bob notes (ten shillings). Oh, how would today's youngsters cope with all that?

Close on the heels of Christmas came the New Year celebrations. Living so close to the town centre, the railways and the docks, there was a cacophony of sound at midnight. From the two railways, the Great Western and the Somerset and Dorset, the trains blew their whistles and from the docks we heard the ships' sirens, whilst the bells of various churches pealed in the New Year.

Very special occasions

The 1950s provided two rather special occasions. The first was the Queen's Coronation in June 1953 when street parties were held across the nation and we had one of our own in Branksome Avenue. Being a cul-de-sac off the main road, it provided a safe haven, not just for our

Branksome Avenue's Coronation street party in 1953. I'm standing just behind and on the left of the cake.

avenue but for the Bath Road neighbours around the corner. The avenue was decked with bunting and trestle tables were spread with jellies, fish-paste sandwiches, fairy cakes and jugs of squash. Being only five years old, my memories of the event are vague, other than that we all had to dress in our best Sunday clothes.

Four years later, the new Blake Bridge across the river was opened and a combined schools' choir performed for the opening. Aged nine, I was supposed to be in it! The best singers from each school were selected and rehearsed the songs to be performed. There were then a series of rehearsals where all the schools got together to practise the combined performance. The day arrived for the first of these and we all piled onto the double-decker bus which was to deliver us. I joined my classmates on the top deck where, amidst all the excitement, we got up to all kinds of tricks, each of us trying to outdo the others. I did a hand stand on the front seat and in so doing discovered that I could 'walk' across the ceiling. Unfortunately, just as I was leaving footprints on the ceiling, the choirmaster popped up onto the top deck to see what the laughter was all about. I was shown the red card and kicked out of the choir!

Work begins on the new Blake Bridge across the river; at the opening I should have been in the combined schools' choir!

4

The Good Life

Waste not – want not

Life was uncomplicated. We lived in a modest home, lacking even basic facilities, rented from a private landlord who could evict us at any time with no reason required, there being no rights of tenancy laws. Initially there was no electricity; we had no bathroom, in fact nor did we have hot water on tap. There was no car to maintain, no deep freeze, no fridge. That meant we had to make do in other ways.

Most memorable of these was the way that milk was handled during the summer months in the absence of a fridge. Our morning milk was delivered to the door by Buster Hawkins. In the summer months he delivered twice a day to reduce the problem of the milk curdling before you had the chance to use it. Buster, wearing his shin-length dairyman's brown coat, would arrive each morning with Prince, his horse, drawing the milk wagon. Mother told us how much milk was needed and we went out with a jug to collect it. Buster's milk was all farm-fresh and held in churns. 'A pint and a half today please, Mr Hawkins,' and Buster would take his long-handled pint ladle, reach down into the churn and pour the contents into the jug, followed by a half-pint ladle's worth. His other measure was the quart (two pints). Whilst my sister held the jug, I gave Prince his morning crust of bread. Milk safely collected, Prince, with no further instruction, walked on to the next customer's house, knowing exactly where to stop having covered the same route for so many years. There was no choice of skimmed or semi-skimmed, simply silver-topped from Friesians or gold-topped from Channel Island cattle.

We all know what happens if you leave milk out for an hour or two in really hot weather, it curdles. Our way to avoid that was to scald the milk as soon as Buster Hawkins delivered it. It was brought to the boil on the gas cooker and then allowed to cool. The skin that formed was skimmed off and used at tea time with jam, as cream. The remainder of the milk was then put into a jug and placed on the cold slab in the walk-in pantry where it would last until the following morning.

If the milk did curdle, it was never wasted. The curdling process was allowed to complete and then the curds placed in an old nylon stocking or piece of muslin. This was hung from a line over the kitchen sink where the whey dripped out until 'cottage cheese' was left in the stocking. We wasted nothing. Stale bread was toasted, using a toasting fork held in front of the fire. Left-over bread went into a bread pudding. Left-over potato and cabbage was turned into 'bubble and squeak' and the dripping fat from roasting a joint or grilling meat stored in a stone jar. Often after toasting stale bread, it was spread with dripping fat which melted into the toast and we sprinkled pepper on top. We called it 'bread and scrape'. I guess it would be seen as unhealthy today but in my childhood we didn't have all those processed foods with high levels of fat. The difference was that we knew what we were eating because all meals began with the basic ingredients, unlike today where you need to read the ingredients on the side of the packet and then know how to interpret 'monosodium glutamates and hydrolysed proteins' into something meaningful. With hindsight, there was very little nourishment in some of our sandwiches. A typical sandwich for me today might contain a thick slice of ham, topped with chutney and salad. As a child it was typically a thin layer of fish paste, or was it just fish-flavoured paste? Sardines soaked in vinegar were, and remain, one of my favourite sandwiches and these always seemed to be on offer at school or church events when a buffet was laid on.

'Sell by', 'use by' and 'best before' dates did not exist. Who needed them? Our food was natural and not stuffed with chemical preservatives, so it didn't keep long. If it wasn't mouldy, we ate it. We didn't need a 'use by date' to tell us whether or not it was fit for purpose. If it was mouldy then, in the case of bread, cheese or similar foods, you cut the mould off and used it up quickly. There was naturally some food which couldn't be eaten, such as vegetable peelings but not even that was left to go to waste. Each household had a silver bin for the pig swill. Once a week the contents were collected, again by a horse-drawn wagon, with a giant silver bin shaped just like a half-round pig sty with doors that rolled up on the sides.

Our meat was kept in a meat 'safe'. This was a simple metal cabinet with a perforated zinc disk, two inches in diameter, in the door to stop the air inside becoming stale. It did little more than keep the flies off the meat. Flies could be a real problem and there were always sticky fly papers hanging in the kitchen. Meat, naturally, was rationed and every household had to register with their butcher, baker, et cetera. That tied you to a particular shop but helped the Government to manage distribution. The butcher could refuse to register you if he didn't want your custom, perhaps if you had a reputation as a bad payer.

Tea was rationed to three ounces of tea per person per week. Whereas most rationing was based on weight, meat rationing was based on value, so the cheaper the cut, the more meat you got. Brisket was popular for this reason but shrank considerably during cooking. The amount of meat available also depended on your relationship with your local butcher. There was often something under the counter for those he knew well and a common request was, 'Is there anything off-ration?' This referred mainly to offal such as tripe, liver and kidneys, but could also refer to unregistered meat. So it never paid to be rude to your butcher for fear that the off-ration meat would be out of stock whenever you were in the shop. Nothing came pre-wrapped, safely sanitised inside polypropylene packing. Instead meat, and likewise fish on the fishmonger's slab, was fully exposed and you could watch the flies crawl all over it. Rationing for meat finally came to an end in the summer of 1954.

Mincemeat was a useful way of using up lower quality cuts and those who knew how to make it keep longer would ask the butcher to mince an onion in with the meat. Rabbits could be bought on a Wednesday morning at the cattle market but once in a while our father would bring one home from the post office. The postmen doing the country rounds would often be given the gift of a rabbit. Those visiting the farms would also be offered a glass of cider and there were some who would visit the farms even when there was no post to deliver!

A joint of meat or a chicken was always expected to provide more than just one meal. Roast chicken on a Sunday would leave enough surplus meat for a second meal, after which the carcass would be used to create a stew. Likewise with joints of meat, these usually came on the bone which was boiled to provide yet another meal and pot-stock for soups and stews.

Tea-time was based around sandwiches. Fish paste thinly smeared on the bread provided a savoury flavour but no nourishment value, whilst sugar sprinkled on the butter provided a sweet but equally low-nourishment alternative. Fritters were another post-war favourite. Fried from a batter made of flour and milk, with an egg thrown in when available, the fritters would contain a slice of spam as a savoury treat, or apple rings or sliced bananas as a dessert, in which case they'd be served with custard.

Food for free – or almost

As children, we were all entitled to free orange juice, which was distributed from the Government food office in the town centre. My sister and I were singled out as examples of healthy children and used in a publicity photo to encourage mothers to take advantage of the free offer. This resulted in me, as a toddler, being seated on the lap of Sir Gerald Wills, the town's Conservative Member of Parliament, much to the horror of my father who was a staunch Labour supporter. Another supplement with which we were provided was cod liver oil with malt extract. It was a real treat to dip a dessertspoon into the jar and slowly twirl it as it was pulled out, ensuring that every last drop was captured.

Although our mother did her best to keep us healthy, she was also a great believer that we should catch every contagious disease going in order to build up our immunities. Hence, if chicken pox was doing the rounds, we'd be encouraged to play with those who had caught it, especially if it was during the summer holidays. So we had chicken pox, measles and mumps with no ill effects. However, in 1957, we were to receive extra rations of orange juice. Asian flu was sweeping the world and killed millions. My sister and I both contracted the virus and were ill for weeks. I can vaguely remember waking up in bed, semi-delirious, to see before me many of the mothers from the avenue gathered around the bottom of my bed. I guess I was in a bad way! But the outcome of the visit was that most of the mothers in the avenue gave up their free orange juice so that Pat and I could make a speedier recovery.

Mr Betty's bakery was just around the corner but we rarely used him. I suspect he was not the cheapest. At the other end of the town was Bowering's, another baker's, but it was worth the walk because they sold penny bags of 'stales'. All bread and bakery products needed to be sold whilst still fresh. Food lacked the preservatives that now get added. At the end of each day, the baker would have a certain amount of left-over items which had to be shifted. A bagful cost a penny. You had to take pot luck as to what you got but that never bothered us. It was usually eaten before we got home and was a favourite stopping-off place on my way home if after-school activities had determined that we would be passing the baker's near closing time. At the grocer's the 'bargain buy' was broken biscuits. Since biscuits didn't come pre-packaged but supplied in large tins or barrels, there were always broken biscuits at the bottom of the tin which were sold at a discount.

In the evenings, food for free was available for the local kids from the fish and chip shop. It was 'scrumps' which cost nothing. These were the odd bits of batter and chips that were left behind when the decent stuff had been sold. It would all end up in the waste bin unless given away. The only cost to the chip shop owner was that of the paper in which it was served but, since fish and chips in those days were wrapped in newspaper,

Bowering's bakery where penny bags of 'stales' could be bought.

it was the lads that collected the newspapers for the chippy that were given the free bags of 'scrumps'.

The fields and hedgerows also provided free food. September was the month for blackberry picking. We walked miles picking from the hedgerows and the farmers never seemed to mind that we were using their fields. It was generally a family affair with mother in charge but it was a different matter if you wanted to help yourself to apples to complete the ingredients for a blackberry and apple pie. That was 'scrumping' or 'snobbing', local names for pinching apples, a practice which our mother would never condone, but to which father would turn a blind eye. That same time of year was also good for picking the large flat-headed field mushrooms where two or three alone would fill a frying pan.

In the spring, dandelion leaves made a good supplement to a salad if lettuce was in short supply. Another springtime commodity was moorhen eggs. They are birds of the ponds and ditches and build their nests on the water, often like a raft attached to a willow branch near the water's edge. Usually with the minimum of wading, the nest could be reached. When we found one, we would mark the eggs in it with a crayon. Moorhens lay an egg a day, just like domestic chickens. Each day we would take the fresh one, leaving the remainder to hatch. The eggs would then be taken home and treated as a normal, albeit smaller egg. There was no protection for birds in those days, other than for really rare species, and in fairness there was such an abundance of wildlife that our collecting could have had little if any impact.

A useful source of protein was caterpillars. Am I joking? Only partly. We were very young, perhaps five or six years old, when Margaret, the eldest of the Manley sisters, came running to us saying that Dilene, her younger sister, was going to die. Margaret had collected a jar of caterpillars and Dilene, not being old enough to know better, had eaten the lot. She suffered no ill effects but it was a 'bush-tucker' trial that was never repeated. We did, however, eat plenty of eels, which were easy to catch with a big lobworm, the sort that comes out onto the lawn at night.

The young eels, elvers, arrive around February each year having travelled the Atlantic from the Sargasso Sea. Ours come up the River Parrett and spread from there across the county, even going cross-country like snakes when they are fully grown. The elvers come up the river on the high tides and are fished for using large nets. In the 1950s, just a few people fished for them and they provided a local food source. Our father sometimes brought them home and mother, having dipped them in flour, fried them and served them up on toast.

Eels, in my childhood, were so abundant that you could not fail to catch them. We used two methods. The first was rod and line, using a large lobworm and fishing on the bottom of almost any pond, canal or river. On one occasion we were fishing a pond near the village of Combwich. The pond was in the middle of a field which conveniently contained a cattle trough. We decided that we would put all the captured eels into the trough to keep them fresh until the end of the day. Sadly, when we returned to the trough, the eels had disappeared, and then we spotted them heading off across the field like snakes searching for a safer place. They may be fish, but cross-country travel is no barrier to these slippery fellows.

The second method was rayballing. This required a large number of lobworms to be threaded onto a length of worsted wool to form a knotted ball. The worm-ball was lowered into the water and left until it could be felt that a large number of eels had attached themselves. The ball was then slowly raised to gently lift the eels out of the water where they were shaken off to drop into a small floating tin bath.

The mud-laden tidal River Parrett proved to be the most bountiful for catching eels. It was easy to catch enough for a meal in under an hour if you went when the high tide was on the turn and the river at its slackest.

Few fish could survive in the muddy river silt so if you caught anything, it was bound to be an eel.

Elver fishing nowadays is big business and a fair amount of it is done illegally. It's serious money with the elvers going to the continent for fish farming and to Japan. Elvers now command upwards from £300 per kilo! Naturally that has to be controlled so you need a licence to fish for elvers. But all you have to do is apply, pay the price and off you go. There is no limit to the number of people fishing for them. Consequently, elver numbers have plummeted and the price has rocketed. That makes them all the more attractive to those who hunt the elvers. Many of the netsmen come down from the Midlands and they are a hard bunch. There is much competition between them and the local lads who, it has to be said, have a bit of a shady reputation. A police inspector once told me that he welcomed the arrival of the elver fishing season because local crime, burglaries in particular, reduced by 30%; the local villains apparently are too busy elver fishing! The end result of this rape of our rivers is that the adult eel population has declined and with them went the otters, whose favourite food is the eel.

Pop goes the ginger beer

Fizzy drinks were seen as an expensive luxury being little more than flavoured, coloured water. Greater fun was derived from making your own ginger beer and many households had a ginger beer plant growing on their window sill. This is not a household plant in the normal sense of the word but a mysterious yeast-based culture which was kept in a large glass jar, or in glass bottles. To this was added water, sugar, lemon juice and ground ginger. The culture grew in the bottle, giving off carbon dioxide and giving the drink its fizz. Normally several bottles would be kept in a cupboard and you knew when it was ready as soon as the first bottle blew its cork. The culture could be split up to create several new plants and hence it became a never-ending process.

Fortunately for us, not everyone made their own fizzy drinks; there were people who bought bottles of Tizer and Corona. The benefit for us kids was that there was money back when you returned the empty bottles. The best ones were the Tizer bottles with the ball and wire clip-on tops which provided 3d for each returned bottle.

Make do and mend

With mother being a dressmaker, much of our clothing was home-made. Starting from the top down, in winter we wore knitted navy-blue balaclava helmets. These were great for keeping out the cold but not a patch on today's thermal wear. As soon as they got wet, they just made the cold weather worse. Coats were always bought much too big, knowing that we'd grow into them. Sleeves were rolled up at the cuffs to compensate. Shirts were worn until they went thin at the collars and cuffs. Once we had worn right through the material, the collars and cuffs were carefully removed, using a 'quick-unpick', turned over and stitched back on. A shirt was never finished until both sides of the collars and cuffs had worn through.

Our trousers, as youngsters, were always shorts held up by an elasticated belt with a snake-design clasp. The flies were always button-flies and I well remember my first pair with a zip fly. My mother had made them for me and was quite proud of them; 'fashionable' she called it. I was horrified. Only girls used zips. Boys at that stage *never* had zips and I just knew I would be the laughing stock of the playground if my secret was discovered.

Our socks were home-knitted and the left-over wool never thrown away, being put to one side for the inevitable repair, using a wooden mushroom which would fit inside the sock making the darning process much easier. They were darned several times before being put out for the rag man. Perhaps because they were home-knitted and had been repaired several times, they were always falling down. The iconic schoolboy image is of a lad with one sock up and one sock down. To counter this, we used garters, usually just wide rubber bands which left an impression on the skin like a car-tyre tread and this took hours to disappear assuming you had kept your socks on all day.

Jumpers, cardigans and jackets would likewise have the elbows patched. Even when clothes had finally had their day, they were either recycled for cleaning materials or kept back for the rag man who would pay a few pence for a bagful. The ultimate embarrassment was the knitted swimming trunks which stood no chance of keeping their shape once wet and became embarrassingly saggy, perhaps achieving twice the length at which they started.

Our shoes had leather tops and soles and to ensure the heels and toes didn't wear out too fast, we had heel and toe protectors, crescent-shaped metal plates which were nailed on at the front and back. They made a loud tap when walking on hard ground and would spark in the dark if you ran and slid along the pavement using your heel as a brake. It was always the heels and soles of shoes which wore out first and the local cobblers' greatest source of income came from their running repairs. It must be decades now since I had a pair of shoes repaired but, in those days, most of the shoes walking around the town would have been repaired at least once. In our garden shed, there was a metal last, a block of steel shaped like two human feet at right angles with a short length of leg attached as a three-legged implement. This would be placed foot uppermost between the cobbler's legs and then a shoe needing repair placed upon it, using the metal shape as an anvil. So whilst father repaired our shoes and mother fixed our clothes, we did our best to wear them out.

Travelling tradesmen

Buster Hawkins with his horse-drawn cart delivered our milk but it was delivery boys on bikes who delivered the bread and meat. The bread was quite light but the poor old butcher boy had to deliver quite heavy loads on his butcher's bike. The basket on the front was so huge that there was only room beneath for a small front wheel. This made steering and balance very difficult. The small wheel exaggerated the turns whilst the heavy weight of the basket made the bike unstable. The bike could never stand up on its own so it came with a large two-legged stand which was used to prop it up when making a delivery.

Once I reached senior school age, I had a delivery round for Mr Pitman, our local butcher. I used to deliver to a large private housing estate and was grateful that the task became easier as the round progressed and the weight in the basket diminished. There was one road where all of us butcher boys were wary. In it lived a massive German shepherd dog, with a dense, shaggy black coat. Resembling a grizzly bear, it wandered its territory unattended. It knew what the butcher boys carried in their large baskets and would stand in the middle of the road, holding its ground, like an ill-tempered border guard, and growling with its eyes narrowed. No one knew what the outcome would be if we didn't pay the toll to get past the beast, so we all carried the ultimate border-guard bribe, a large knuckle bone which would keep him occupied long enough for us to finish our deliveries beyond the range of his canine radar.

At the end of the summer, the French onion sellers came across the Channel, via Plymouth or Weymouth, with strings of onions hanging from the handlebars of their bikes. The bicycled knife-grinder was another annual visitor. He could prop up his bike so that the back wheel

A Hercules-brand butcher's bike, difficult to steer and to balance.

was off the ground. That was connected by a belt to a grinding wheel attached to the handle bars. Sitting astride the bike, he would pedal away and sharpen items on his grinding wheel. My mother always gave him her dressmaking scissors, garden shears and our kitchen knives. He also knew that he could expect a feed at our house and so timed his deliveries for the lunch hour. That way, he got fed and mother got preferential rates.

We had travelling tinkers who repaired pots and pans, and gypsies who sold 'lucky white heather' at the door which mother always declined, but erring on the side of safety to avoid the gypsy's curse, she always bought some of their clothes pegs. These they made by hand, cutting willow from the local hedgerows, shaping them into the two halves of the peg and then binding them with metal strips cut from old tin cans. The tinkers and gypsies came with flat-bed wagons drawn by their palomino or piebald ponies. The rag and bone man was another who came with horse and cart, heralding his arrival by loudly calling, 'Rag and bone – rag and bone!' as he rang his hand-bell. He bought the rags which we could no longer use. The bones he purchased went to the glue factory. We even sold our old newspapers and any scrap metal, collecting what we could from generous neighbours. It was only a few pence at a time but it was pretty well the only pocket money we got.

In between these unpredictable visits, my mother often got me to take a load of old newspapers, rags, empty bottles or scrap metal down to 'Sammy's'. Sammy Roberts was the owner of a scrap-metal yard in nearby

The knife grinder's rear wheel was raised, connected by a belt to the grinding wheel near the handlebars.

Polden Street and if you've ever seen a TV episode of *Steptoe and Son*, it was just like that. I'd walk in carrying the bundle of whatever it was we were looking to convert to cash and Sammy would place it on the huge set of scales. Sammy would part with his cash and I'd go home feeling like a regular wheeler-dealer.

Our coal also arrived by horse and cart. Our main source of heat was from the open fire and this meant having a good stock of coal and logs through the winter. Unlike today where coal seems to be very clean and safely sealed in manageable plastic sacks, our coal was delivered in hessian sacks which leaked the plentiful dust. The coal man was always black from head to foot by the time he reached us, wearing his leather skull cap with a long flap which ran down over the back of his neck. Needless to say, it was an intensely dirty job, worse even than that of the chimney sweep. Almost every home had a coal fire, or perhaps logs or peat, so sweeping the chimney was an annual ritual, unless you were prepared to run the risk of a chimney fire. All the kids in the street would gather in the middle of the road, looking skywards, watching for the sweep's brush to pop up from the chimney pot, at which point a huge cheer broke out and the sweep, inside the house, would know that the job was done. He'd then pull the brush down a couple of feet until it disappeared, only to pop it back up again a few more times, just to add to the fun. The soot removed was spread on the back garden so all the terraces of houses in our part of the town had jet black soil.

5

Tea-slurping Grannies

Did everybody's grandmother slurp their tea from their saucers or was it just both of mine? Now, I'm not posh by any means but it made my toes curl to watch them. Nonetheless, I count my blessings because at least they lived long enough for me to remember them. I knew neither of my grandfathers, both dying before I was born. In fact, my father's father died when my father was just a year old and his sister two years. My Bridgwater-born grandmother had met and married a Welshman who dug clay in the Somerset brickyards in the summer and dug coal in the Taff Valley during the winter. It was in South Wales that he died, two agonising days after a mining disaster. The family were chapel-goers and my father was baptised on his father's coffin immediately prior to the funeral. My grandmother faced life with two young children and no breadwinner, so she walked the fifteen miles from Treforest down to Cardiff with her few belongings and her two children. There she took passage on a coal boat to the docks in Bridgwater; her father being a mariner, it was probably her father's ship on which she made her return.

She was a tough lady, hardened by life's experiences. When I was in my early twenties, I stood for election to the local council in the ward where at least five generations of my family had lived. My father was well-known, as was his mother. As I went door to door, canvassing for support, voters would ask, 'Are you Bill Evans's boy?' When I replied that I was, inevitably they would respond with, 'I remember your grandmother. God, she had a loud mouth. When it was dinner time and she called your dad home, you could hear her voice the other side of the town bridge!' They elected me nonetheless.

Workhouse stigma

She was a very practical lady and not much of a one for throwing a party. One Christmas, her gifts to our family included a blanket for me and a sack of potatoes for my mother! She had known hard times – very hard times. I once spoke with an old man who lived in her street at the same time and he spoke of the depression years when children died of malnutrition. He had tears in his eyes as he recalled one family who went to their child's funeral with the child in a cardboard box and I wondered if it was his own child of which he spoke. Those were the days of the Union workhouse where in Bridgwater, one third of the inmates died in one winter alone. That same winter the death rate in prison was only three per cent. The workhouse was the last place anyone would want to go. Married couples with no means of support would finish their days there, separated with men in one section, women in another. My grandmother's generation still lived in fear of the workhouse. It was there she died.

In truth, it was no longer the workhouse but a council-run home for the elderly. In my grandmother's final years, she suffered poor health and was virtually bedridden. She would stay with us for six months, and then with my father's sister for six months. It was during one stay with my Auntie Sis that my aunt decided her mother should go into a home, Northgate Lodge. That was its official title but everyone in Bridgwater still knew it as the old workhouse. The ambulancemen

The Northgate workhouse, a place of dread to the elderly.

arrived to transport her to her new home but she refused to go. She was terrified. They dragged her into the street kicking and screaming. A butcher boy who knew my family was passing. 'Run and fetch our Bill!' my grandmother cried. The ambulancemen agreed to wait until my father arrived. He was furious, not having been consulted. The ambulancemen were sent away and my grandmother came back to stay with us. The winter came and went; summer arrived. We were going off on a summer holiday. Our grandmother went to stay with our aunt for a week.

The second day that she was there, my aunt had her taken into Northgate Lodge where she died the next day. It began a family feud between my father and his sister, a feud which they took to their graves. When my father was seriously ill, and we were preparing for the worst, his sister refused to visit him. He recovered and outlived his sister. She died intestate and the lawyers had to resolve the issue of the inheritance from her estate, which in a nutshell was a house. Father received the letter notifying him of his inheritance. He read it angrily and threw it on the fire. He refused to accept it.

Of course, the solicitors were obliged to hand it over to him but were struggling. A couple of years passed by with a succession of legal letters despatched to the flames. In time, the solicitors decided to sell the house and pass the proceeds on to my father. This they did – but he treated the cheques the same way as their earlier letters. He just kept throwing them onto the fire. The interest was growing and with each new cheque, at roughly six-monthly intervals, his inheritance was even greater than the last time. He grew angrier. 'Why can't they just give it away?' In the end, we persuaded him that if it were to be given away, it had to be him that did it. The solicitors could only act on his instructions. 'If you know so much, you sort it out!' he yelled. So we did. Mother banked the cheque and a rainy day fund had been set aside. He was a very stubborn man, just like his mother before him, and just like my daughter. I'm so glad it missed a generation!

Everybody's granny

My mother's parents both had the toughest start to their lives. Each of them had been born in a workhouse, my grandfather in the Helston workhouse in Cornwall, my grandmother in Plympton St Maurice near Plymouth. Everybody in our avenue knew her as Granny Richards. Raised in Cornwall, she had learnt many of the old country ways and was full of words of wisdom and superstitions. She never allowed May

Granny Richards with me and my older sister Pat.

blossom in the house, nor peacock feathers, nor new shoes on a table, et cetera. The list was endless. But she was also a fount of knowledge regarding old cures and remedies. She produced oil of cloves for toothache, a bowl of steaming water with camphor oil to clear a chest, and various other cures using nature's bounty.

The two cures which remain the strongest of my memories involved the removal of warts. The first cure, which was the simplest to put into effect, was to pick the stem of a dandelion (ignoring old wives' tales about this causing bed-wetting), and use the dense white sap which seeps from the stem, applying it to the area of the wart. Do that three times a day for two or three weeks, and the wart miraculously disappears. It gets stranger. If the dandelion fails, then try the toad method! Take a large toad (country folk always knew where to find one), wrap it in a waxy leaf, like a rhododendron, and keep the leaf around the toad for a day. You then remove the leaf and bury the toad in loose soil. It is important that the toad can dig itself out – but not too quickly. Meanwhile, take the leaf and apply it to the wart and keep it there until the toad has escaped, typically the following day. The wart will eventually fade away.

Believe that? Well, I did because it was my grandmother who told us. When I attended grammar school and developed a liking for the sciences, I learned to discount her silly country remedies. But we ignore these pearls of wisdom at our peril. I was about thirteen years old when a classmate was suffering with an annoying wart which he kept knocking. Our biology master advised him that, at our twice-weekly lessons, he should take the small bottle of silver nitrate (which we used to test for the presence of chlorine in water), turn it upside down to wet the cork, and use the cork to apply the chemical to the wart. In two or three weeks the wart would disappear. I believed him because he was my biology master but no longer believed in my grandmother's cures. Nonetheless I told him about my grandmother's folklore and he then put me straight. If you go to the chemist to buy wart remover, it contains silver nitrate – that's what does the business with the wart. The dense white sap in a dandelion stem also contains silver nitrate. My grandmother's cure really worked although she never knew why or how, just that it did.

Decades later, I was listening to a Radio 4 science programme. The subject was cancer and new developments for cures. Scientists had discovered that toads can secrete a chemical from their skins which attacks cancer cells. The chemical is used as a deterrent to predators. If you wrap a toad in a waxy leaf, the wax absorbs the chemical which you can then apply to the wart, which is effectively a type of cancerous growth. Granny Richards knew this all along, not how but just that it did. One of my greatest regrets in life is that she died when I was just five years old. If only she could have lived long enough to pass on further knowledge, and if only I had had the wisdom at the time to take her knowledge at face value, then I would be a wiser individual. When she wasn't busy curing warts, she would tell fortunes and predict the sex of an unborn child. This she did by dowsing, using a ring or needle suspended on a cotton thread. At least I managed to inherit her dowsing skills.

Her final gift to me was a pop gun. She had promised me one for my sixth birthday but knew that she was dying. She sent my mother out to buy one and was able to give it to me before she died. My birthday came four months early that year. I count my blessings that I have happy memories of her and that I have had the benefit of living long enough to watch my own grandchildren grow well beyond the age that I was when my last grandparent departed.

6

School Days

The first days

My first day at school arrived. It was a short walk from our home to the Eastover infants' school. As newcomers, we were taken first to our classroom where we were each given a set of building blocks and were told to build a tower. This was presumably to assess our level of ability. It was an easy task and I soon had a neatly-aligned set of blocks which the lad next to me promptly knocked down. My father had told me to stand up for myself if anyone tried to bully me and convinced me that, no matter how big the other lad, it gets easier if you fight back; otherwise you become a regular victim for the bullies. The teacher pulled us apart when I retaliated and it was my first lesson in not getting caught.

My second lesson was not far behind. We were all taken into the school hall to be introduced to the routine of morning assembly. We formed up in rows as instructed. Mrs Perrot, the headmistress, stood at the front and told us to close our eyes and put our hands together as we prayed. Dutifully I put my hands together but kept my eyes open, keen to take in my new surroundings. I had never seen the point in closing eyes for prayers. I never did in church and no one chastised me there, but Mrs Perrot told me that if I couldn't close my eyes, I would have to leave the assembly. So close on the heels of the episode with the tower of blocks, I decided that school wasn't the place for me and promptly left. I walked home alone, unimpressed with my first day. It all seemed a waste of time, building up tower blocks for other kids to knock down and having to close your eyes when you are actually trying to learn about your new surroundings. When it was realised that I had disappeared, my sister was sent to drag me back.

Beyond that first day, I have few memories of my days in the infants, in contrast to those in the juniors where my memories are much clearer. I can recall how we were issued with pencils for which we were responsible. When the lead was blunt, we had to seek the teacher's permission to sharpen it using the sharpener which was bolted to her desk. We played hide-and-seek a great deal but since the only place to hide was around the back of the coal shed, the game never lasted very long. Piggy-in-the-middle was popular and involved three players; piggy was the one who stood between the two others as they threw the ball back and forth between them until piggy eventually caught it, in which case piggy swapped places with the last one to throw the ball and so the game continued.

At least there were no canings in the infants' school; that came three years later when we progressed to the juniors. The headmaster there was Mr Hook who had only one arm, having lost the other in the First World War. Every Armistice Day, he would get us all into the playground to stand for two minutes' silence. The deputy head was George Bell and I'm glad it was him who dished out the punishment for errant lads. I was still just short of eight years old and the bully, now in his final year, was almost three years older than me. We had been warned that each of us lads in turn would have to face the bully's music. I was both the youngest and the smallest in my class. The situation was not looking promising. Sure enough, before we had been in the juniors for more than a week, it came to my turn. He was massively bigger than me. Somehow I managed to get around behind him, leap up onto his back, grab him and hold him around the neck as tight as I could with one arm whilst flailing him with the other. I didn't dare let go. I knew that as long as I could keep behind him, I'd be okay but face-to-face I'd be mincemeat.

Before too long, and none too soon for me, the playground monitors intervened and dragged us off to the deputy head's office where we stood outside the door waiting to be called in. The monitors entered; the door closed as they made their report. As they left, George Bell called for the bully to enter and I was told to wait outside. From within I could hear his angry voice as he told the bully that he would not tolerate such behaviour. I could hear the threatening swish of his cane as he paced the room. All then fell silent, briefly. Next came the sound I had been dreading, the swish followed by the smack of the cane as it made contact with the bully's rear end. Whack, another, then another, followed by three more; six of the best. The door opened; the bully with head lowered returned to his classroom. I was called in.

'Well, young Evans, I hear you defended yourself quite well!' I was confused. His attitude towards me was quite friendly and calling me by my surname seemed odd. The teachers in the primary school always called us by our Christian names. 'Well done, lad, but try and keep out of trouble if you can. Off you go then, back to your classroom.' And it was all over – no caning. I didn't understand.

My next problem was that I knew I'd have to tell my parents what had happened. If I didn't, someone else would. For certain, if I had got the cane at school, my father would have clipped me around the ear for getting into trouble even if it wasn't my fault. When he arrived home, I told him the full story. He smiled and said, 'There's no way George would have caned you. Me and George shared a desk together at the same school, grew up together, played rugby for Bridgwater and Albion together, skittled for the same team. You'll never get the cane while he's in control.' It all fell into place.

I was, however, able to return the favour albeit I didn't realise it until many years later. Every now and again, our teacher would swap us around in respect of whom we sat next to in class. Shortly after the punch-up incident, I was moved to sit next to Peggy Bell and she remained my desk partner for most of the remainder of my time at the school. I was regarded as a bright child at school and was particularly strong in mathematics. It was Peggy's weaker subject and so she was able to benefit from sitting next to me. Years after I left school, I bumped into Peggy and she commented about the arrangement. It was only then that I realised that she was George Bell's niece.

One of the many changes between the infant and junior schools was the progression from pencils and crayons to ink and paints, the latter only used in art lessons. Each classroom had an ink monitor, me being one of them. Our desks had lift-up lids beneath which we kept our books and in the top-right corner of the desk was a hole in which sat the inkwell. Running across the top of the desk was a shallow half-round groove where our pens were placed when not in use. The ink pens had wooden handles and a metal nib, split along the tip. The nib was dipped in the well and then the thickness of the writing determined by how hard you applied the nib to the paper. Every few words, you needed to re-dip the nib into the ink and then be careful to keep it point down for fear that the ink would run back onto your fingers. The fingertips of our writing hands always seemed to be ink-stained. The role of the ink monitor was to mix fresh ink from 'Stephen's Blue-Black' powder each morning and top up the wells.

Melting the milk, coconut mats and frozen toilets

Morning lessons were interrupted by mid-morning milk, each schoolchild in the country being allotted a free one-third of a pint of full-cream milk. Pre-war poverty and wartime rationing had left a nation of less than fully fit children and so the Government had introduced free school milk. There was many a family whose children would go to school with a layer of cardboard in their shoes to cover up the holes in the soles and you only had to look at them to know they were undernourished and probably never got milk at home.

The milk arrived each morning in wire crates. In the summer months, by the time the milk was issued to the class, the metal-foil milk bottle tops would already have been opened by the blue tits who had long since learnt where to find the cream. In contrast, in the winter months the milk would arrive frozen and the first duty for the class's milk monitor was to put the crate on the classroom stove, a cast-iron coal burner. There the milk would thaw, pushing off the tin-foil lids as it did so.

In similar fashion, when the weather got really cold, the water cisterns in the outdoor toilets froze solid, perhaps for days. We had no indoor toilets, and school would be closed for the duration. We loved the cold weather if only for that reason. If it rained and froze, the playground became our ice rink. There was never any attempt to salt it to render it safe. We simply used it as a skate park.

Lunchtimes followed a routine. We ate our lunches and then had to lie down for half an hour on coconut mats. These were hard and bristly, the bristles irritating the back of your neck. We had to lie flat on our backs and keep straight, with our arms at our sides. We tried to shuffle up the mats to get our heads onto the hard floor rather than the bristles but were always ordered to get back on the mat 'properly' and keep our eyes closed. Meanwhile, the dinner ladies or teachers walked up and down between the lines of children to ensure all obeyed the rules. My sister remembers one occasion where she lay on her mat angrily looking down at her 'Utility' shoes, black leather with laces. Other girls had started to wear shoes with straps and Pat was becoming fashion conscious!

Although school milk was free, school meals had to be paid for at a shilling a day. The first thing on a Monday morning, our teacher called the register and each of us in turn walked to the front of the class and handed in our five shillings for the week. Children from poorer families were provided with free school meals. The process of handing in your dinner money was another potential humiliation for those who had nothing to pay as it singled them out from the rest.

Our form master, Mr Burton, was particularly enthusiastic about nature and it certainly rubbed off on me. Being a town-centre school, our exposure to nature study was down to seeing whatever Mr Burton decided to bring in. In the spring, there was always a tank of tadpoles in the corner of the room so that we could witness them develop into frogs.

In Mr Burton's classroom; his love of nature rubbed off on me.

We were given jam jars which we lined with blotting paper (an absolute necessity when working with old-fashioned ink) and put soil within that. Between the glass jar and the blotting paper we would place a pea or bean seed so that we could watch it push out its shoots and roots as it developed.

The nit nurse and other cultural issues

A regular visitor to our primary school was the 'nit nurse' in her long brown coat and matching felt cap. Her mission in life seemed to be to humiliate any poor soul who had dared to enter the hallowed grounds of one of her schools carrying head lice. In the 1950s, head lice infestations were a regular problem and many a young lad had a crew cut as one means of reducing the risk. Those discovered with lice were sent home immediately and not allowed to return to school until the problem had cleared. In most families it never happened or perhaps just the once; but there were some families who were regular offenders and in the worst cases this could result in being sent to the 'clinic' where all the hair was cut off and then the scalp treated. The children were then allowed to return to school, the girls wearing a head scarf.

Whenever there was an outbreak of nits, we were given a note to take home to our mother and although the note never named the offending family, everyone knew who they were – because they were banned from school, hence the humiliation. Then in countless homes, out came the nit combs and the sheets of newspaper over which your hair was combed. Heads tipped forward, we would stare at the sheet hoping the unwelcome invaders didn't appear in our household. Meanwhile, out in the streets could be seen children with greasy, smelly hair having had the nit-destroying lotion applied, and knowing that everyone else knew that they were 'lousy'. There is a different attitude to head lice these days: 'No one dies of head lice – their education is far more important.'

Although there was no school uniform, we all wore short trousers and long grey socks. This was the tail-end of Utility clothing. We were at such an age that we often grew out of clothes before they were worn out, in which case we passed them on. We were all working-class kids and we all wore hand-me-down clothes, but some were worse off than others. Some arrived at school wearing daps (plimsolls) because there was no money to buy leather shoes, even during the winter months.

Elocution lessons and the absence of Germans

My mother was keen that both my sister and I should do as well as possible at school. She had grown up in Cornwall and was allowed to sit the eleven-plus examination which could gain her access to the grammar school, some eight miles from her home. The problem came when she passed but the family could not afford for her to go. She was determined that we would not fall victim to the same poverty trap. Towards that end, there were always plenty of books in the home. We were also both encouraged to use the town's library, which we did with much enthusiasm. She bought us dictionaries and encyclopedias. I remember clearly one particular children's encyclopedia which was published just after the war. It had one section specifically about the war but surprisingly there was no mention of the Germans and Japanese, only the Allies. How can you have a war without an enemy? It reflected the anti-German and Japanese feeling that prevailed at the time.

As another way to guarantee a smooth road to the grammar school, mother paid for me to receive private coaching in how to pass the eleven-plus and for my sister and me to receive elocution lessons. These were provided under the auspices of the Co-operative Society for the children of working-class folk and we attended these semi-private lessons on a weekly basis; but it wasn't everyone's cup of tea. Angela, our friend and neighbour from next door, also came along but couldn't handle the lessons without rolling into fits of laughter. She was never cut out to talk posh, I don't suppose any of us were, but Angela's sense of humour proved to be a real barrier. Each week we would be given a piece of text to practise ready for the following week's lesson. Angela's problem came to a head when the text was about life on board a ship. Unfortunately, the ship concerned had a 'poop' deck and the killer line of poetry was:

The gull swooped on the dusty poop.

On reading this line, Angela simply fell apart. She never, ever managed to finish the poem, collapsing into fits of hysterical laughter. She was a hard act to follow; once the giggles have started, they are hard to switch off.

The school playground

At junior school, we lacked basic playground facilities. There was no grass area, just tarmac. The playground was split into two naturally separate areas, one for the girls, who had climbing bars, and the other for the boys, who had nothing except white goal posts painted onto red-brick walls. We seemed to spend most of our playtimes playing 'war' games, sometimes cowboys and Indians, making appropriate whooping sounds if we were on the side of the redskins, but more frequently with one side being the Germans and the other the British. Having no toys for weapons, we acted as though we actually held machine guns and made the appropriate noise: 'ack-ack-ack-ack'. We all knew the sound of a Tommy gun and the whistle of an incoming shell. 'You're dead, I'm not' was the popular phrase. Whereas children today are encouraged not to have toy guns or play violent games, we were weaned on them. We also repeatedly sang songs about Hitler and his lack of body parts!

It must be remembered that our fathers, overwhelmingly, would have spent six years or more of their lives in active service, fighting the Germans, Italians or Japanese. Many lost family members and close friends, killed in action. Look at any war memorial today and you are looking at a reminder of our history. For the parents of my generation, it had been a part of their lives and there was little love for the Germans. It was natural for them to watch us play these 'character building' games of playground war. If it wasn't war, then it was football with a tennis ball or British Bulldog, a game where one lad stands in the middle of the playground whilst every other boy stands in a line against a wall on one boundary of the play area. The idea is that every child on one side of the playground has to run across and touch the wall on the other side. The job of the boy in the middle is to stop them. It wasn't easy so the lone lad realistically had to target perhaps the smallest or slowest of the 'enemy' and capture him, after which the captive had to be lifted so that his feet were off the ground whilst the captor shouts 'Bulldog'. Then there are two in the middle and gradually the game gets easier until there is only one boy left to capture. He is the winner, and the next Bulldog.

In contrast, over in the girls' playground, they would tuck their skirts into their knickers and swing upside down on the play bars or join in the skipping games with their inevitable rhymes, 'Salt, pepper, vinegar, mustard'. These skipping games were played with a long rope and a girl at each end. They would start with one girl skipping in the middle and others would join in. Somehow it involved numbers, as if learning the times tables by rote, and often the lines 'Never mind the weather girls; all in together girls'. But that was a different world and one we were not allowed to enter.

'Chase' or 'Tag' was played in both playgrounds although we called it 'It'. Someone was nominated to be 'It' and they would chase anyone else in the game until they touched (tagged) them and then that person became 'It' and it was their turn to chase. A variation of this was 'Off-ground It' where you could not be tagged if you were off the ground, perhaps standing on a milk crate or hanging from the play bars. This 'sanctuary' was only allowed for a limited time; you couldn't stay there forever. The game was also played outside of the school when boys and girls played together in 'Kiss Chase'. The convention here was for a boy to chase a girl, or vice versa, and once the prey was tagged, a kiss was exchanged to seal the deal. Boys of junior school age hated being kissed by girls and generally would outrun them, but learnt to run not so fast as they got older!

Playtimes always ended with the ringing of the hand-held school bell at which point several boys would make a dash for the toilets, which meant less time to be spent in lessons. At one stage, this practice became so annoying to the teachers, that the playground monitor was instructed to block the entrance to the toilet before ringing the bell. The boys had to learn to go during playtime and not class time. It only took one afternoon of sitting with crossed legs to learn the lesson.

7

Child's Play

Clowning around!

When the circus came to town, it was a huge event to which everyone was bound to go. Its arrival was well publicised. We all knew what time the specially-adapted train would arrive and living so near the railway station, we all headed off to watch. It was Bertram Mills's world-famous circus, which arrived at one side of the town and had to make its way to the Fairfield on the other side. Before leaving the railway sidings, the elephants were bedecked in scarlet and gold robes whilst stilt walkers and jugglers donned their costumes. Spontaneous laughter broke out as the elephants stuck their trunks into the pockets of the railway staff to pinch their packed lunches, no doubt placed there by the circus staff as part of their routine. As a publicity spectacle it worked and we were all taken to see our first big top performance.

Everyone knew when the Bertram Mills Circus came to town.

We were only about four or five years old at the time. My best friend, David, and I went to the circus with our mothers and each came away with lasting impressions. Dave had been fascinated by the clowns and their hilarious antics. I was most impressed by the cowboy and Indian show where the cowboys magically lassoed the Indians. On returning to the avenue, and with tea safely out of the way, we played our circus games.

First it was clowns, the result of which was that I ended up drenched from head to foot after Dave had thrown a bucket of water over me. My revenge came by pure accident. I was the cowboy, Dave was the Indian. The lasso was made from an old clothes line with which I had fashioned a sliding noose. Having amazingly managed to reproduce the cowboy's dexterity, I hurled the rope successfully over David's head and then reeled him in. The circus cowboy had tied his captive Indian to a totem pole. In my case, I tied Dave to a railing which ran along the top of the wall at the bottom of the avenue. I tightened the rope. It was old rope which was beginning to fray, and having tightened was not prepared to slacken. Efforts to release the tension only caused the noose to tighten even further. Unfortunately, it was around Dave's neck and I soon realised that the game was not going according to plan when his face began to go blue. We were rescued by our mothers who heard Dave's desperate and somewhat stifled pleas for help. I was taken home for a change of clothes and Dave was whipped away to recover. Neither of us was allowed out for the rest of that day but normal service resumed the morning after.

Cocky Five Stones

One of our street games was 'Cocky Five Stones'. All you needed was a ball that bounced well and any stones you could find in the street. The game began with each of us holding five stones in our cupped hand. The hand was then flipped and the stones caught on the back of the hand, then flipped again to catch as many stones as possible back in the palm of the hand. The person catching the most would be the one to start the game. With five stones each, we'd put them all in a central pool on the pavement. The one to go first would bounce the ball and then grab as many stones as possible, plus the ball, before the ball bounced for a second time. The ball would then be passed to the next player who would do likewise. When everyone had taken a turn, the one with the most stones would set the rules for the next game; perhaps two bounces would be allowed, or ten stones each, or a forfeit to be paid for catching fewer than a given number.

'Cocky Five Stones' was typical of the many games we played in that there was no expense involved other than the cost of the ball. Marbles was another. These could be bought for a few pence a dozen. Ball bearings from old machinery came free of charge and were actually much better than the glass marbles. These games reflected the complete absence of surplus income; we made our own games and used our imaginations to greater effect. We had pea shooters made from the stalks of cow parsley which was hollow down the middle and just the right bore to take unripened elderberries when they were still green and hard, or hawthorn berries if the stalks were big enough.

Wet weather never stopped our play and provided fresh opportunities such as matchstick races using the rainwater which flowed down the road gutters before disappearing into the drain. There were always plenty of spent matchsticks in our houses, most appliances depending on gas rather than electricity, and so we would use the discarded matchsticks to race them down the gutter in an urban version of 'Pooh Sticks'.

With the main Bristol to Exeter railway line so close to our home, the railway soon became part of our extended playground. There didn't seem to be the fear in those days of children playing on the line. In the beginning, our games simply consisted of waiting for the train signals to change, at which point we would rush to the centre of the bridge and stand over the line as the train passed beneath, enveloping us in a cloud of steam. We were only five or six years old but within a year or two we had found our way down the embankment and would place pennies on the line to see how flat and enlarged we could get them. By the time we were eight or nine, we were confident enough to use the British Railways trackside telephones to speak to the man in the signal box. It all depended as to who was on duty as to whether we had a friendly chat or the threat of police action!

None of us ever came to any harm, the survival instinct was too strong and somehow there was never the need to play 'chicken'. The only fatality I remember, other than the occasional rail disaster, came when a man committed suicide near the local station. He simply walked out in front of a straight-through train. In the morning we were told that his arm had landed in the school playground. We unsuccessfully spent the lunch hour hoping to find yet to-be-discovered bits!

Collecting cigarette cards was a popular pastime and this promotional concept was extended to tea cards, each packet containing a free card. Typically there'd be 20 or 50 cards to a set which could feature cinema stars, footballing legends, England cricketers, World War ll fighter aircraft, Royal Navy ships, British birds, butterflies, et cetera. It was important to get the album to collect these in and then to get every auntie, uncle and friend of the family to switch their loyalty to PG Tips or whichever brand was giving away the cards. Then, at school, we would have 'swapsie' sessions where we exchanged our duplicates to fill the gaps in our collections.

We also collected car numbers, which sounds stupid now but consider the trainspotting fraternity! When we were lads of four or five years old and had just been learning our letters and numbers, there were very few cars. In a morning's car spotting, you could collect as many as 30 or 40 numbers. The following morning we'd be back there again only to discover that, with the exception of perhaps one or two new ones, the cars were all the same ones we'd seen the previous day.

A 'chequered' past

We also collected cheques. Not far from our home, the local Cellophane factory had purchased a disused clay pit and used it to dump their waste, including lots of official paperwork. In those days, every financial transaction was done by cheque or cash. Large companies could get through thousands of cheques and these ended up in the landfill rubbish. It was quite easy to get into the tip area, just slipping under the fence, and there we would collect the cheques, always looking for the high value ones. We were probably no more than six or seven years old at the time.

Playing around the pits in theory could be quite dangerous. They were deep and more than one child drowned in them. There was one such pit which had actually been a dry dock at one time, where the last wooden ketch to be launched from Bridgwater had been built. It was here that one of our close friends drowned when sadly there were none of us there to help him. Shortly after, the council had the pit filled in.

Equally dangerous were the docks, not that we ever saw the danger, simply the fascination of the ships from faraway lands with crews who spoke in foreign tongues. Most of the dock traffic was coastal shipping bringing coal from South Wales but there were timber boats from Scandinavia and Poland, and coal boats from Germany and Russia. We would try to talk with the crew whose knowledge of English was crude but just enough for all concerned to have a good laugh. Although perhaps they shouldn't have encouraged us to linger around the dockside, I guess we reminded them of the families they were missing at home. One boat permanently resident in the docks was *Bertha*, the dredger designed by Brunel. Relentlessly she ploughed her way up and down the docks, dragging the silt which collected at the bottom of the basin up to the lock gates where it could be flushed out on a low tide.

Living so near the river, we were always aware of the tides and what that meant for the tidal bore which sweeps its way up the river twice daily. In the spring and autumn, these tidal waves could be a foot or two high and

Bertha *the dredger, ploughing her way up and down the docks, and the Swedish MS* Westa *at the dockside.*

on the high spring tides we had regular and predictable flooding in the town centre. A visit to the town centre today will reveal a high wall all the way along the river to prevent flooding but in my childhood, we took the floods in our stride. My wife is the eldest of nine children who all attended the local Roman Catholic school which was a matter of yards from the river bank. Most homes in the town kept a tide timetable, hers included. Each morning during the flood-risk period, her mother would check the tables for the times and height of the tide and from that make the decision as to whether her flock would wear shoes or wellington boots to school, knowing the only access to the school was frequently through the flood water.

On yer bike

We rarely saw a car in our avenue and so cycling was quite safe. Even on the main road, cars were quite rare. The surrounding land was totally flat and so almost everybody rode a bike. Many a child's Christmas present was a brand-new, second-hand bike. There wasn't much money around so a new bike was out of the question. Second-hand bikes were purchased and hidden in the garden shed where the father of the family rubbed the paintwork down to the metal using emery cloth prior to giving it a fresh coat of paint. It took hours but time they had, money they did not. You just couldn't imagine anyone going to such trouble today. And there were no such things as fashion bikes: no BMX or mountain bikes, no

Binford Place flooded at high tide; most Bridgwater homes kept a tide table handy.
(Courtesy of Douglas Allen)

stunt or folding bikes, just the standard sit-up-and-beg models. Since a
bike was expected to last you several years, as youngsters our 'new' bikes
were always much too big for us. The seat was adjusted to its lowest
possible position and then blocks of wood attached to either side of the
pedals until the pedals were fat enough that our little legs could reach
them. It mattered not that we couldn't touch the ground as long as we
could reach the pedals. As our legs grew, so the blocks came off.

When my sister and I were still quite young, we decided we would cycle
the 26 miles to Minehead. Mother put her foot down, declaring it to be
too far and unsafe. So we cycled to Cheddar instead. That was 20 miles –
but we only told mother once we were safely home. From then on, we
were rarely seen without our bikes.

No boundaries to our playground

Our 1957 move from a low-grade terraced town-centre home to a newly-
built council house on the edge of the town presented us with a
completely different world in which to play. Our semi-detached house was
one of a new development and we were the first family to move in. All
along our road, new houses were under construction on this boundary
between town and country. At night we built dens using stacks of bricks
and kept the cold at bay by lighting fires in old oil drums, using off-cuts of
timber which littered the site. Jack Longman, the night-watchman, never
bothered us as long as we weren't doing any damage. As it turned out, he

was a drinking buddy of my father and when we needed some timber for shelving in our new home, Jack was the provider. During his overnight rounds, he lobbed a dozen lengths of timber over the hedge into the neighbouring field. The following morning, my father woke me nice and early with instructions to go into the field, find the timber and lob it back over the hedge but this time into our back garden.

Within weeks of moving in, my best friend Dave had moved in just around the corner. At ten years old, we began to discover the countryside. We built tree dens and made bows from hazel branches and arrows from the willow. They were pretty useless but they were grist to our vivid imaginations. As we explored the fields and hedgerows, moving deeper into the surrounding countryside, we discovered the magic of derelict river barges and the lizards that sheltered within, ancient orchards in which barn owls nested in old trees and Jenny Wrens in their ivy. We fished for tadpoles, newts, minnows and sticklebacks in the ditches and rhynes. All of these have long since disappeared, as has the range of flora in the fields which flooded with each winter's rain, where skylarks and lapwings built their nests in the spring. We learnt to fish and spent countless days sitting at the water's edge watching bank voles, or water rats as we knew them, whilst waiting for our floats to give a tell-tale dip. Our first fishing rods were simply branches from the hedgerow, with cotton and a bent pin. All we caught was small fry but it had whetted our appetites and we soon took to coarse fishing with a passion and before long had saved up to buy decent rods and tackle.

Life was full of adventures. We built rafts using old scaffolding planks and oil drums which we'd take from the building site. On one trip to a disused clay pit, another gang of lads nicked our raft and paddled their way out to a small island in the middle of the pond, but we had the last laugh. We'd not built the raft particularly well. As they stepped ashore, the barrels parted company and, picked up by a slight breeze, drifted away. The rival gang had to swim back.

Some months later, Kipper Martin and I were fishing for newts in a small pond which was in the very centre of a field, and fortunately had a number of well-established willow trees around its bank. It was fortunate because we had failed to notice the herd of cows approaching us. Under normal circumstances, this wouldn't have been a problem but these Friesians had just been polled, a process where their horns are burnt off. They were in a foul mood and galloped towards us for the attack. We were young and agile enough to quickly scramble up the willows where we were obliged to remain for what felt like an hour, until the cattle drifted far enough away for us to sprint to the field gate.

Just across the lane from that adventure was an old orchard in which was a low brick-built barn. In the late autumn, the barn was used to produce cider. This centuries-old process involves chopping up the cider apples and then squeezing the juice out of them in a cider press. The juice is used to produce the cider and the pomace which is left, being the residue of the apple, is fed to the pigs. On this occasion, the pomace had been left in an old tin bath and it had rained for several days leaving a few inches of rainwater in the bath. The pomace had soaked up the rain water and fermentation had started. When the sow was brought into the orchard, she devoured the apple pomace and munched her way down to the bottom over the course of a couple of days. By that time the juice in the bottom had turned to rough cider which she consumed with relish, leaving her totally intoxicated. We watched her as she stumbled, fell, got back onto her feet until she crashed into the barn wall which she then used as her only means of reliable support. Leaning into the wall, she took careful step after careful step until reaching the end of the wall. The moment her means of support ran out, she simply keeled over onto her back and slept it off for the rest of the afternoon.

Ditch jumping and wasp nests

I guess if you spend enough time pushing the limits, every now and then you will pay the price. The fields near our homes were on the flat lands of Sedgemoor, separated by hawthorn and blackberry hedges or ditches and rhynes. Tree climbing was great fun, only once in a while spoilt by falling out. That can be particularly painful if you fall into a hawthorn hedge or blackberry bush. Just before my cousin's wedding, we were playing a game to see who could create the biggest splash in a nearby stream. This involved carrying stones as high up as we could into a tree. As the game progressed, to beat the previous best splash, we had to carry even bigger stones even higher. I was stood below when friend Peter lost his balance near the top of the tree and dropped the boulder. Two hours later I was at my cousin's wedding with three stitches in my head.

Another adventure requiring stitches came when we had a battle with a gang of lads from the other side of the town. Our estate was on the east side of the River Parrett and we frequently played along the east bank of the river, close to where the railway bridge crosses it. Lads from the rival Hamp estate in similar fashion frequented the other side. Once in a while it would be agreed by intermediaries that we would have a battle between the two estates. On one memorable occasion, we found ourselves on one bank of the river whilst the rival gang was on the other. The river was just wide enough to be able to throw stones across and a stone fight commenced. If you've ever watched newsreel footage of youths in Gaza or on the West Bank hurling stones, you can imagine what our skirmish looked like. It escalated somewhat when part-bricks and catapults were introduced.

I never saw it coming. Out of the blue, I was hit just below the left eye with half a brick. Blood was pouring down my face. We jumped on our bikes and headed off to the hospital which conveniently was on our side of the river and less than a mile away. In the hospital, the nurse took one look at the cut and declared it needed stitching. As a twelve year old, I was quite proud of the swastika-shaped scar it left. Fifty years on, the scar has gone but the swastika shape can still be felt beneath the surface. She was a friendly, smiling nurse with a sense of humour. She told me that I needed an anti-tetanus injection and another to prevent blood poisoning. I was asked to roll my trousers up to my thighs, but this was the days of drain-pipe trousers. I couldn't raise them above my shins. She smiled as she looked at me with a twinkle in her eye and said, 'Drop 'em, lad.' I was so embarrassed but it was one of those moments when you realise the validity of your mother's pearls of wisdom when she says, 'No, put clean underpants on. What if you get run over by a bus and you've got dirty underwear!'

We often climbed trees just to get from one field to another. The alternative (we seemed reluctant to use the field gates) was to jump the ditches (not too difficult) or the rhynes (difficult!). Now the rhynes are not only wider, at about six feet or more across, but they are deep and steep-sided; misjudge the distance and fall short of the top of the bank, and you'll hit the side wall of the rhyne and commence the inevitable slide down into the murky water.

Early November brought the bonfire season and most households put back old timber, cardboard boxes, piles of newspaper and so on ready for the bonfire boys to come calling. We also scoured the fields for fallen tree branches. We were about eleven years old when we found one which was too big to carry home so my friend Dave decided to chop it into two. He had only swung the axe half a dozen times when he sliced straight into a wasp nest. They were not happy! The huge swarm seemed to know that it was him and not the rest of us that had rent their nest asunder. He was covered from head to foot in stinging wasps and we were soon running back to my house where my mother stripped off his clothing and doused him in vinegar. Poor Dave was blessed with curly hair which made the task of removing the wasps all the more difficult. Despite the setback, the bonfire was a great success, as it proved to be for many years to come. Each gang of lads had their own bonfire and this frequently resulted in raids on each other's collection of combustible matter.

On Guy Fawkes night we would light the bonfire and then stand back as it flared up before settling down to a manageable level. After an hour or so, the glowing embers around the edges would be pushed in towards the centre where they were used to roast jacket potatoes. We used no protective wrapping such as tin foil, we simply lobbed the potatoes in whole and raked the ashes up around them. You just had to make sure that you used only very large potatoes because the outer quarter of an inch would be completely inedible. Nor did we soften them with butter or serve them up with a choice of fillings. We just ate them as they were, scooping out the soft centres with our knives, and they were wonderful!

Occasionally we threw something on the bonfire that we shouldn't and usually we knew exactly what we were doing. A favourite trick was to find an empty one-gallon can, the sort used for car oil. We made sure the screw cap was tightly in place to provide a perfect seal, put some water inside and then threw the can onto the bonfire. We did this the following morning for two reasons. Our bonfires were large enough that there was still a good heat the following day, but there were very few people around and certainly no adults to stop us playing foolish games. We would throw the oil cans onto the fire and then stand well back. As the water boiled inside, the pressure would build up until the can exploded. The way this worked was that the seam down the side of the can would be the weak point where the can would burst with such pressure that the sides would open wide, with the top of the can attached to one edge and the bottom to the other. Now, rent asunder and shaped like a Maltese Cross, it would rocket up into the air spinning like a helicopter blade. The other reason for doing this in the morning was that you could see the results of the experiment whereas the dramatic flight would have been lost in the darkness and you could not predict where the flying debris would land.

Our trips into the countryside always left us with hearty appetites which we often satisfied whilst still out in the fields. In the autumn, there were plenty of blackberries and apples which we would pinch from the cider orchards. The commonest cider apple in our area was the Kingston Black, sharp and bitter and quite inedible, but the Morgan Sweet, which produced an earlier and lighter cider, was quite delicious. Now and again we were spotted by the farmer who chased us off but was never fast enough to catch us. Years later in adult life, I witnessed an episode where a farmer was giving chase to some youngsters in exactly the same circumstances. The kids outran him and escaped laughing. I then realised he too was laughing and it dawned on me that in all those lucky escapes, the farmer never really wanted to catch us.

8

Off to the Big School

No one was surprised when I passed the eleven-plus. Roger Richards (now Dr Richards) and I were considered the brightest two prospects for some years and if my memory serves me well, it had been a long time since two boys from Eastover had passed in the same year. Others had never been in doubt, as a result of which my nickname at school was 'The Professor'. Whilst this may sound flattering, it is less so when the background is understood. At the time there was a television programme called *The Army Game* starring Alfie Bass, Bill Fraser and many other well-known names. These included Charles Hawtrey, whose character was Private 'Professor' Hatchett. Known to his Hut 29 mates as The Prof, he was the highly-intelligent but equally weedy character who helped them in their schemes to do as little as possible during their time as conscripts.

The eleven-plus behind me, my first day at the Dr Morgan's Grammar School for Boys arrived. I donned my uniform – red blazer and matching red cap – and headed off to school. My mother had always predicted that I would wear a red jacket before I grew up, but this was a reference to the other option which was to go to Borstal, a corrective institute for the worst of the nation's young offenders. It was based on the same military lines as the National Service where you 'make them or

With my sister Pat – all ready for senior school.

break them' whilst introducing them to a system of obedience and respect for authority. Happily it was Dr Morgan's and not Borstal for me.

I arrived at the side entrance to the school where we were told to assemble. A number of senior boys were there to meet and greet us, one of whom stepped forward from the group and walked towards me. Never taking his eyes off me, he picked me up by the ears as he said 'Welcome to Dr Morgan's, young Evans.' I was starting to believe that Borstal may have been preferable! The lad concerned was the son of my father's friend Bill Chidgey, who had been told to 'look after me'.

A public school ethos

Further culture shocks followed in rapid succession. We were introduced to our form master and it soon became apparent that we were there for one reason only, to gain the maximum number of GCE 'O' and 'A' levels. Charlie Keys, the headmaster, ran the school with a public school ethos, strict discipline and only surnames to be used. This was a stark contrast to primary school where we were all called by our Christian names. At the grammar school, all the masters referred to us by our surnames and we were told to speak to each other likewise. Even at the end of the minimum five years we spent together, most of those boys were still known by their surnames.

The headmaster had high expectations of us. We were to achieve a high number of 'O' levels but not by the easiest route. At the local college, they used the Associated Examining Board for the GCEs because

Dr Morgan's Grammar School for Boys, which provided something of a culture shock for an 11-year-old. (Courtesy of Bill King)

73

they were the easiest to pass. We used the Cambridge board because it was the toughest and somehow that made them worth more! When applying for jobs, employers only wanted to know how many GCEs you had, not which examining board was used. But our head wanted his boys to go on to university and there it mattered. He was a somewhat ethereal character, drifting into classes unannounced, simply standing and watching as he jangled keys in his pocket before drifting out again. On one of his drifting days, he wandered out to the swimming pool, stood at its edge and stared at the waters, contemplating how much teaching time should be given over to swimming, rather than to academic studies, which was where his real passion lay. He drifted into the classroom and ordered the class to stand. Raising his arms before him, he formed a circular sweeping motion with his hands and instructed all before him to do the same. The whole class followed his actions as though it were a game of 'Simon says'. Exercise complete, he studied the boys and declared, 'There you are. Since the human body cannot help but float, you can all now swim,' with which he once more drifted away.

Although he was the head, the real power-base lay with his deputy, Jack Lawrence, who walked the school grounds with his camel-hair coat and French beret. Discipline was strict and Jack was the one who applied it, especially where canings were required, which fortunately were rare. The mere threat of it as a punishment was a sufficient deterrent for it rarely to be used. Expulsions were also exceedingly rare. It was recognised by all boys that attendance at the grammar school was a privilege not to be squandered. However, in cases of breach of discipline or a lack of respect for the masters, the individual masters had their own unique techniques for class-control, including a range of weaponry. We had a sports master, Miles Stanton, who used an abandoned plimsoll. This was particularly well used when we were playing 'pirates' which involved dashing from one piece of gymnasium equipment to another without being caught, a variation of tag in which the master had the additional teaching aid of a plimsoll! 'Snoz' Coates would hurl a board rubber at any offending boy and even continued this practice after the occasion on which the target youth ducked and the board rubber went through the glass window. There was a physics master who used a length of rubber tubing which he would whirl around in the air like a musical propeller, earning it the nickname of Whistling Willy. 'Trog' Ansdell, our art master, used a wooden spoon. Others used a ruler and one had a block of wood with holes drilled in it, apparently to make it lighter and easier to wield. I still wonder whether the headmaster was aware of the existence of these weapons.

Weapons of class destruction

Most feared of all our masters was Glyn Rees, who we all grew to love and respect and still talk of fondly today. He was our metalwork master, was proudly Welsh and had a hair-trigger temper. He would fly off the handle at the drop of a hat and throw the nearest metal-working tool which came to hand. The only defence was to lift the lid of your desk at just the right moment. He was also famous for his unique technique for handling end-of-term exams. These were always based on a written paper and not on practical work, so each term we had the same set of questions: 'Write down all you know about files and filing'; 'Write down all you know about screws and their types.' Your written paperwork, now available in case a school inspector appeared, was then stored away and ignored. The real assessment then began.

'Right, boys, line up in the order you came at the end of last term.' Once we had sorted ourselves out, he would point at us one by one saying, 'You, boy. Move up two places. You – move down one.' In this fashion he would rearrange our end of term results until he was satisfied with the hand he had dealt us. We all understood the logic to the process which was nothing to do with metalwork. He was very musical and taught violin. When I commenced violin lessons, I moved up five places in one go. When I dropped the violin, I moved back one space per term until I found my more natural level. If you sang in the choir at St Mary's church, if he knew your mother, if... And that was how it worked. He would then point at the first boy and say '90', the next was 89, then 88 and so on until each boy had been issued with his final percentage mark for that term's exam.

When we finally took our GCE metalwork practical exam, we were each given a number of pieces of metal which had to be cut, shaped and assembled to look like a tuning fork with a tapped thread running down through the centre of the handle. The invigilator for these exams was Vaughan-Jones, the English master. He would sit back in the corner to ensure no boy cheated. Glyn Rees then gave him a newspaper to read and he would disappear behind it for the duration. Now although I was strong in some subjects, I was not too good at metalwork and as we approached the end of the allotted time, Glyn Rees wandered around looking for any boys who clearly were not going to finish. I almost panicked when I realised that a particular component of my yet-to-be assembled masterpiece had disappeared. I quietly caught Glyn's attention. He looked and winked and said, 'Don't worry, boy. It'll be back in a minute.' Unbeknown to me, while I wasn't looking, he had taken the piece into his workroom where he drilled the hole and tapped the

The metalwork shop at Dr Morgan's, where we attempted to hone our engineering skills. (Courtesy of Bill King)

thread. All I had to do was fit the bits together. No one who took metalwork under his guidance ever failed the metalwork exam and I now understood why. It has left me with a bit of a conscience. When people asked how many 'O' levels I had, I always said eight, not nine!

Decades later, long after the demise of grammar schools, I was one of a group of old boys who started the Dr Morgan's Association, the purpose of which was to organise an annual reunion dinner. We had already arranged an after-dinner speaker when Glyn asked if he could address the 'boys' once more, to let them know what it was like during the war. Now the 'boys' were all 50-plus, and Glyn was well into his nineties. I agreed he could speak to the boys as a pre-dinner speaker. You could have heard a pin drop as he related the story of how the Americans had supplied the RAF with machine-gun bullets, but the bullets were the wrong gauge to fit the British guns. They needed to be milled down and so Glyn and his metalwork students were charged with the task. He was fiercely proud of his achievements in that, during test-firing over the Bristol Channel, not one of the bullets adjusted by his boys misfired.

He then continued to tell us how, on one occasion, he had returned from the store room to see that one of his boys had placed a live round in a vice. The boy had a metalworker's punch in one hand and a hammer in the other and was about to detonate the bullet. He could have killed himself or anyone else in the room. Glyn's face lit up as he told us, 'You know, boys, I picked up the first thing to hand, a wooden mallet and I threw it at the boy!' A huge cheer raised the rafters as we all reflected on the numerous occasions we had seen him behave in similar fashion but in less serious circumstances. He then continued, 'And that was the only time in my whole career in education that I threw anything at one of my pupils.' The laughter that erupted lasted several minutes. I put my arm around his shoulder and thanked him. His face was aglow. A matter of months later I related that humorous moment when I delivered the eulogy at his funeral.

I have previously mentioned Vaughan-Jones, who carried the nickname of Bonzo. He always wore a black gown and had the habit of leaning back against the blackboard, slowly obliterating anything he had previously chalked up. At the end of the lesson, he would leave the classroom and walk along the corridor closely followed by a vapour trail of chalk dust. I remember our very first lesson with him. All the masters in those early sessions emphasised that we were there to gain academic qualifications. Bonzo emphasised the importance of good English and how lucky we were to be in this privileged position at the Grammar School. 'You boys have been selected as the cream of the district. However, my first impressions suggest that this year's intake is clotted cream!' He taught us English language and was more proficient in the mornings than the afternoons. It was his practice to visit the West India House during the lunch hours and was noticeably less coherent and certainly less tolerant on some afternoons. He was nonetheless an effective albeit fastidious teacher. In his own mild way, he seemed to enjoy inflicting short-lived pain on his pupils. To provide just one of many examples: he would slowly pace up and down between the desks delivering his message and then select a boy at random to see who was paying attention. It was after one of his West India House sessions when he stopped just behind me and caught hold of my ear, twisting it quite hard as he asked, 'What is a gerund, boy?' Although experiencing the pain of an ear being increasingly twisted, I felt a wave of relief since I knew the exact answer he wanted. 'It's a verbal noun, sir,' I replied. 'That's right, boy,' he said as he twisted my ear even harder. I couldn't believe what was happening. I gave the right answer and the pain got worse.

I got my own back. We were asked to write an essay about schoolmasters and I wrote about him and the ear twisting episode. When our homework was handed back, mine was unmarked and was delivered with the message, 'You will see me after class.' I stood alone at his desk as he told me that the essay was not only unacceptable but that he demanded a written apology. I impertinently asked if there were any grammatical or syntactical errors in my essay because I felt it was well written. 'Don't be impertinent, boy. I'll have a written apology by tomorrow or you'll be sent to see the head.' 'I'll be happy to see the head, sir,' was my response.

I knew that if he had to present my essay to the head, it would raise questions about his afternoon performance level and the way he treated the pupils. I had a complete class of witnesses who would hopefully confirm that what was written was true. The following day arrived and I still refused to apologise. I was given until the end of the week, then the end of the month, half term and the end of term. After that it went unmentioned. He bore no malice, which surprised me and decades later I know that my knowledge of the English language benefited no end from his ability to teach.

When we returned to school after the summer break, Bonzo was using a walking stick. The story then unfolded as we were told that on the last day of the previous term, after his extended lunchtime visit to the West India House, he had failed to safely board his train to Taunton, having put his foot into the gap between the platform and the carriage!

He was a good teacher; it was just his methods which were unconventional. We all recognised that the teachers with whom we were blessed were an exceptional team. They were enthusiastic and professional, supportive and caring. We couldn't have asked for better.

Bert Bollom taught us French and was another beret-wearing character. I did quite well at French and at the end of one term examination managed to answer ten out of ten questions correctly. When we were given our percentage marks which would go into our school reports for our parents to see, I saw that I had been awarded 99% and not the 100% I expected for getting ten out of ten correct. I was sat in the front row of the class at the time and questioned the master with, 'How come I only get 99% when I got every answer right?' He replied, 'Because no one is perfect, Evans.' I retorted with, 'Yes, but for the questions I was set, I did give the perfect answers.' '98%, Evans! Any further discussion?'

Extra-curricular activities

Apart from the regular and expected sporting activities, the school was blessed with a Fives court, another example of the public school ethos. This was a game similar in many ways to squash but was played in the open air within the bounds of three brick walls. The red leather-covered ball was 'batted' against the far wall using the palm of the gloved hand.

Projecting from a side wall was a buttress behind which the ball could become trapped. It was a fast and furious game. Close to the Fives court was the swimming pool with its two low diving boards.

These were just some of the recognised activities. A less frequent one was the dance classes where we were taught ballroom dancing. Now, in a school which is all boys, it was impossible to find a female partner and so, once in a while, we would march down to the girls' grammar school where an equal number of girls would line up along one side of the hall whilst we lined the other. Nervously we would eye our potential partners on the other side of the hall, determining which ones we would avoid like the plague, whilst they did the same staring at us. On the given command, we were told to find a partner and then the dance lessons began.

This process was repeated in life outside of the school if we went to a church or village hall dance. Lined up along one side, with no time pressure on us, we would eye the girls opposite and choose a target. Now, unlike school dances where a girl had to dance with you if asked, in these less formal dances, the girl could always decline your request. That was the unnerving aspect. We would discuss whom we fancied and goad each other into taking the first step across the dance floor. Once you had started your move, there was no turning back. We walked across the floor as casually and confidently as we could portray whilst churning around inside. Then came the moment of truth; you ask her to dance and she smiles or coyly flutters her eyes in agreement, or she looks at you like a piece of dirt and says, 'No, thank you' if you're lucky or 'Not on your Nelly' if you're not and you commence the long walk of shame back to your side of the hall, feeling the humiliation as your so-called friends chuckle, until they realise it's their turn.

Amongst the clandestine school activities was the smoking club, of which I was a member. Our headquarters were at the back of the school cricket pavilion. There was a loose plank around the back, out of sight of the school buildings. When lifted, this allowed a hand to pass through and slide the bolt to open the door giving access to the small back room in which were kept the cricket nets. Here we hid away during our lunch breaks. As far as we knew, we went through our entire time at Dr Morgan's without being discovered. Decades later, at a dinner where I was sat next to Bernard Storer, our biology master, I mentioned the smoking club and how we were never discovered. 'What do you mean never discovered?' he said. 'There was you, Harris, Smith...' and he rattled off the complete membership. It transpired that they knew all along but figured that as long as we were out of sight on school premises, we wouldn't go wandering off the campus.

The very best of masters

Bernard Storer and Mal Davies, our biology and sports masters respectively, were great characters. On a week's canoeing trip down the River Wye, they were the two masters in charge. We were aged about thirteen and well below the legal age for smoking – but we did so nonetheless. Dick Sperring was a particularly large chap and not designed for fitting into or getting in and out of canoes. At the end of one day's canoeing, Dick did the inevitable. He was caught with one foot on the bank and the other in the canoe as the two moved further apart. With a gentle and quite graceful descent, he sank into the river. His fags were a soggy disintegrating mass. The two masters felt so sorry for him, they gave him ten cigarettes from their own supplies. Wonderful chaps, respected and loved by all.

In a further incident on that same expedition, I was sharing a double canoe with Mal Davies. We had just the one double, all the others being singles, and it was my day to double up with the sports master. We were approaching a fast-running rapid when we both realised we would hit the rocks unless one of us got out to lighten the load and allow the canoe to sit higher in the water. Now Mal Davies, being the full-grown adult, leapt out and stood shin deep in the centre of the river with the waters of the rapids swirling all around him. Meanwhile, in the now lighter canoe, I shot the rapid down into safer water. The trouble was I needed to go back up the river, paddling back up over the rapid, to recover my abandoned PE master. The first two attempts proved fruitless as the power of the water snatched me first to the left and then to the right in my vain attempts to pick him up on my way past. You could see the irritation on his face as the useless English boy shot past this athletic son of Wales. However, it was third time lucky and we were reunited. To my embarrassment, the next copy of the school magazine had a report written by Mal Davies giving his version of the episode and stating, 'My only consolation was that I was standing on Welsh soil.'

A further humorous incident occurred on one of our sports days when Mal Davies was in the gym organising the boys prior to their events and Jack Lawrence, the deputy head, was acting as the official out on the race track. To add a sense of importance to the occasion, Jack was using a proper starting pistol. Every few minutes, Mal would hear the crack of the pistol as another event got underway. Then a breathless boy dashed into the gymnasium declaring to his sports master that the deputy head had shot one of the boys, Sidafin. Mal rushed to the scene of the crime only to discover that Sidafin had fallen over on the starting line the very moment the gun was fired.

There was a lad in our class called John Bottomley who died sadly far too young, in tragic circumstances. But during his school years he was quite a character, brilliant at art, geography and history but dreadful at anything sporting. Whilst most of us carried satchels to school, Bottomley had to be different; he carried a briefcase, a proper job – strong leather and with a substantial lock. He was an absolute master at avoiding PE. In the absence of a note from his parents, he would find some excuse: 'Please, sir, I've forgotten my daps', 'Please, sir, I've forgotten my shorts', or his T-shirt or anything that got him out of PE. Then came the day when he remembered every last bit of kit required and had no note from mum. He beamed as he proudly told Mal Davies that, at long last, he had finally brought all his kit as he placed the lockable briefcase before him to provide the evidence. 'Well done, Bottomley,' said Mal. 'Now go and get changed.' 'Can't, sir,' came the reply, 'I've forgotten the key.'

In later life, I was once heckled by Bernard Storer when I was after-dinner speaker at a school reunion. We had a four-house system whereby each of us belonged to Fairfax (my house), Wyndham, Cromwell or Hopton. These were all characters from the English Civil War. At the previous year's dinner, the guest speaker had spoken at length about the success of the boys who were in Wyndham house. I decided to entitle my talk 'Fairfax strikes back' and I commenced by discussing the seedier side of the historic Wyndham family. I quoted an example of a Wyndham who stood for Parliament and was found guilty of vote rigging by bribery and intimidation. Then I related the story of Lady Crystabella Wyndham who, during the siege of Bridgwater Castle, exposed one of her breasts to Cromwell as an insult. She had been the wet nurse to the infant Charles ll. She was also responsible for teaching him the practical art of love-making just before his 15th birthday. Imagine that! I commented on that with, 'What a way to be taught sex at school. We never had lessons like that!' A voice from the audience shouted, 'Didn't you listen to anything I taught you in biology, young Evans?' It was the voice of Bernard Storer.

We had some great characters in our year. There was one chap who had a passion for chemistry and he loved experiments with a hint of danger. He collected small amounts of chemicals from the chemistry laboratory until he had enough for his purposes. In one experiment, which was presumably successful from his point of view, he blew the lock off the door of the public toilets on the nearby Fairfield. I can only imagine that either he became a chemist at the nearby Royal Ordnance factory or a safe-breaker; probably the latter. He was that sort of character.

SOMERSET BORN, SOMERSET BRED

Cross-country running

Rugby was the school's winter sport. Following the principle that rugby is a game for hooligans played by gentlemen, and football is a game for gentlemen played by hooligans, we were not allowed to play football. Well, that's not quite true. Football wasn't banned as such, but footballs were. We were allowed to take any sort of ball into the school, to be used during the mid-morning and dinner breaks, as long as those larger than a cricket ball were oval in shape. So we could play football with a tennis ball or a rugby ball, but not a football! Some of the lads were quite good at football and played for their village sides but this was frowned upon and best not mentioned.

I much preferred long-distance running. We had some excellent cross-country runners in the school, many of whom ran in the national schools' competitions. In my class, I had the ability of occasionally coming third, a position with which I was quite happy. In our first year at the school, we went off on a cross-country run which involved running across fields before reaching a quiet road and then a mile or so back along the road. It was a hot summer's day and I had just got onto the road stretch when, just for fun, I stuck out my thumb to hitch a lift, not seriously believing that I would be picked up. The nice lady pulled up, smiled and invited me to jump aboard. She told me how she always felt sorry for the young boys from the grammar school when she saw them on their cross-country runs, so she was quite happy to give me a lift and drop me at the school gates. Panic set in as I realised I was now passing all the boys at the head of the field. I explained that I would much prefer to be dropped just up the road from the school, outside the West India public house. There I could slip behind a large tree and then emerge into my favoured third place. 'No, no,' she continued, 'it's no problem. I'll take you right up to the school.' And that is what she did.

It was an embarrassing moment as I stepped out of the car and thanked her kindly for the lift. There was the sports master, Mal Davies, waiting for the first arrivals and there was I, a good five minutes ahead of the best of them. To my amazement, I got away with it. 'Today a boy showed initiative and came back ahead of the rest of the field. The next time it happens, it will be copying and the boy concerned will be punished!'

He was a lovely master who always had an awareness of what was going on and had a great sense of humour. Some years later, we were about to embark on another cross-country run when the usual character, who is best left nameless, produced the note from his mother to say he had to be excused PE. A short distance into the cross-country course was a ditch which we had to cross and the safest way when the water wasn't too deep,

82

was to jump into the water at the bottom of the ditch and scramble up the other side. To help the runners to extricate themselves from the ditch, any boys excused PE would be sent via a gate around to the other side of the ditch to help haul the runners out. On this particular day, it was just the one lad and he just happened to be the least popular of our group. John Chadwick and I were the first to reach the ditch, into which we jumped. We had pre-planned that we would each hold up a hand at the same time to be hauled from the ditch. This we did and the excused boy held one hand out to each of us. The inevitable happened and instead of us being hauled out, the excused lad was hauled in.

Still amused by the situation and having completed the run, we returned to the school and took our shower. It was important to get to the shower early. It was a communal shower consisting of two rows of showers heads forming an aisle. It came as a culture shock for many when they joined the school because we all stripped off and went in together, naked. There were one or two boys who couldn't handle it and never took the shower. However, with the shower finished, it was time to go home. I went to the bike shed to discover that my bike had disappeared. We never locked bikes in those days – they never got stolen. I went to Mal Davies, the sports master, and explained that my bike had disappeared. 'Don't worry, young Evans. It seems that one of your class got pulled into the ditch so I had to send him home early. I let him borrow your bike to do it!' He was a wise and astute master and I had a long walk to collect my bike.

The school gym at Dr Morgan's. (Courtesy of Bill King)

Those who found it uncomfortable to enter the communal shower must have found the visit by a school nurse an even more traumatic experience. We were all told to line up outside the library where the nurse would see each of us in turn. We were at the age of puberty and were about to be checked to ensure that both of our testicles had dropped. It was short and sweet, a quick grope by the nurse behind a modesty screen and then, with a sigh of relief, off to the other end of the library for an eye-sight test. For those of us in the queue outside, word soon came back as to the nature of the medical – 'A nurse will fondle your testicles.' 'Hell's teeth,' we collectively thought. 'God!' said one boy. 'What if I get an erection?' We were all fearing exactly the same potential embarrassment. 'Don't worry,' came the answer, 'She's seen it all before. She just whacks it with a pencil.' Just the thought of having your best friend whacked with a pencil was enough to make it behave when the moment came.

The trip to Venice

'Trog' Ansdell, being the art master, organised a school trip to Venice. I was aged thirteen and was extremely privileged to be able to go. I imagine that, although I know my mother had to pay something, it must have been heavily subsidised since there was no way our family could have afforded such a trip. It was a memorable journey involving a train journey across France, through Switzerland and down into northern Italy. We changed trains in Milan where we were able to buy really cheap bottles of Chianti. For the price of a bottle of Tizer, we were picking up our first-ever bottles of wine. Not knowing the strength, most of us had finished our bottles by the time we reached Venice. As I stepped off the train, after 36 hours of travelling and a bottle of Chianti, I could feel the ground beneath my feet swaying. Most of us could. Trog explained that this was the effect of spending such a long time on a moving train. More likely than not, it was the Chianti because the experience was not repeated on our return trip.

We had an excursion in a gondola during which the attractive female tour guide snuggled ever closer to Trog at one end of the boat whilst the gondolier serenaded us with romantic Italian songs. It seemed to be doing the trick for the tour guide but Trog was clearly concerned about his reputation. The singing came to an end as the gondolier asked, 'Hey, whya don'ta youa boysa singa a songa for mea?' This was just the distraction Trog needed to take his mind off the now limpet-like guide. 'OK, boys. Sing up.' 'What shall we sing, sir?' 'Anything, boys. Just sing.' We gave them all ten verses of 'Ten green bottles' as Trog shrank in embarrassment and the tour guide slowly sidled away back to her own side of the seat.

9

What Did You Do in the War, Dad?

Most boys at school could tell you what their dads did in the war. It was still very fresh in their minds. We were always conscious of the effect the war had on some of the fathers. One had a full head of white hair although he was still only in his thirties. Another had a high-pitched squeaky voice which made him sound somewhat childish. They had both been prisoners-of–war in the Japanese camps. We heard the horror stories and knew that you would never hear the victims themselves relate the tales of their traumas.

Children can be cruel, especially where disabilities are concerned, but we all felt humbled in the presence of those who, through no fault of their own, carried the visible scars of war. There was a need for boys to know that their fathers had seen action and not been cowards. There was a need to know that they stood and faced the enemy, so most lads had stories about their father's own experiences. Sadly, my father refused to talk about it and so I could never join in the 'What our dads did in the war' debates. When questioned, his stock reply was, 'Those that saw the least, talk the most about it.' Perhaps I should have been able to read between the lines but I only understood many years later. I did once get him to say, 'Look, son, all I did was to help keep the roads clear. That's all.'

I imagined him with a donkey jacket, wellington boots and spade, like a navvy, in contrast to other boys' fathers carrying their rifles at the ready. He did once, in an outburst of anger, give a clue to at least one of his experiences. We were in our teens and had just watched an American war film. My best mate, Dave, then explained to my father how it was clear that John Wayne had won the war single-handed. He loved winding up my father, especially about the Americans; we all knew how he hated them. His reaction was completely unexpected. It was the first time I heard my father swear in anger. In a short outburst, he related a situation where he was facing an advancing German army. He and his colleagues were under instructions to hold back the German advance long enough for the Allied troops to effect an orderly withdrawal. Retreating in chaos costs far more lives than an orderly withdrawal. The British troops held their positions well, as did a US black regiment, but the white Americans picked up their weapons and ran despite instructions to fight to the last. My father's reaction was to let go with a burst of machine-gun fire across the front of the retreating Americans, with the message, 'Hold your positions or we'll shoot you as well as the ******* Germans!' His purpose in relating the tale was not to let me know what he had done but to explain his opinion of the American fighting-machine.

That was the only clue that he had seen action but I was to find out in later years just what he meant by 'keeping the roads clear'. He was just short of 80 years old when he died and it was seven years after that when I delivered a talk for the Blake Museum Society in Bridgwater. Bill Chidgey was the chairman of the society and it fell on his shoulders to do the vote of thanks for my talk on Bridgwater Fairs and Markets. During the talk, I used 35mm slides to illustrate the subject and amongst the images was a picture of a fairground boxer standing at the front of the boxing booth, pummelling away on a speedball suspended from the roof. I talked of my memories of my father as a fairground boxer and wrestler. As it happened, Bill Chidgey had worked for decades with my father as a postman and they knew each other well. Bill related how, on the occasion of his honeymoon in the 1930s, he and his bride had cycled on a tandem down to Barnstaple in North Devon. There they visited the fair and watched my father box.

It was a bit of a surprise to hear someone talk about one of my father's performances but it was a shadow of the surprise about to be delivered. Bill continued, 'That wasn't the only time I saw Roger's father in an unexpected place. During the war, when I was in the Paras, I was air-dropped into North Africa and got separated from my unit. I managed to find an area where British troops were operating and linked up with them, hoping eventually to find my way back. I was given a plate of food and a hot drink and was asked in a friendly manner where I was from. Bridgwater, I said. I was then told that they had a Bridgwater bloke with them. "Do you know Ginger Evans?" they asked. "Know him?" I said, "I work with him." It looked as though I'd be spending the next couple of days with them so they asked if I would like to go and find him. When I agreed, we jumped into the back of a truck and went eight miles down the road and there we found Roger's father, Ginger Evans. He was busy clearing landmines.'

It was then that I realised just what my father meant when he said, 'Look, son, all I did was to help keep the roads clear. That's all.' I reflected on his other stock answer: 'Those that saw the least, talk the most about it.' It raised even bigger questions about his experiences which I knew would now never be answered.

Another one of his expressions was, 'If you're not scared, you're not enjoying yourself.' This was such a contrast to the man who in his later years was a close friend of the armchair, but in his younger days, even well into middle-age, he had led a very active life. Born in 1909, he was in the Navy by the time he was 14 years old. He travelled most of the world and learned to box and wrestle. He could even claim to have been the one-time boxing champion of the Yangtze River. This was in the years between the wars when the British, French and USA all had their fleets up the Yangtze to protect their commercial interests in China. A real 'small world' experience came when he won the title from Harry Elson. Harry was another Bridgwater man and his nephew was my best friend David. My father had also been a keen footballer and played in a scratch England side against a Dutch team in the six months after the war when he was still clearing landmines in Holland. He was in Holland during the final years of the war and I guess I'll never find out what he was up to but I know that, on one visit home, my mother stitched bicycle inner tubes into the hems of his army uniform so that he could smuggle them into Holland to help a Dutch family who had befriended him. Other clues of his war-time experiences came from some of the useful foreign phrases he taught me, those he had learnt during the war. I soon knew the German for 'Hands up' and 'Where is your commander?', and the French for 'Will you walk with me?', 'Close the door' and 'It doesn't matter.' Clearly he had learnt to capture the Germans and woo the French!

My father had been a 'top man' on pylon construction between the wars, all the way from Bristol to Bodmin. He was one of that rare breed that climbed to the top of the giant pylons when the power cables were being installed down into the West Country. He even played rugby at Murrayfield and Twickenham when he was in the Navy. After the war, he settled down to the quiet life of a postman, perhaps because he was married and with a young family but maybe he'd already crammed too many adventures into one lifetime.

10

A Walk on the Wild Side

Where town meets the country

The facilities in our Branksome Avenue home were poor and the rent was high, the house being owned by a private landlord who could charge whatever he liked. We had been on the council waiting list for some years and eventually reached the top. This coincided with brand new council homes being built on the eastern edge of Bridgwater, on the Sydenham Estate. The day finally arrived when we packed all of our belongings into the back of a lorry, mum and dad sitting up the front with the driver, my sister Pat and me standing in the back of the lorry, looking over the top of the tail-gate, with the neighbours waving goodbye.

It could have been a sad departure, leaving close friends behind, but we knew that they too would soon be making a similar journey. The Snooks family, Auntie Doll and Uncle Bob from next door, moved into a house right across the road from us, and the Elson family, including best friend David, moved to just around the corner. Life continued much as before but with some significant differences. Most notable was the change of culture; no longer were doors left unlocked; neighbours no longer popped into each other's houses with a 'Coo-ee' as an introduction; families kept to themselves. The camaraderie and neighbourly spirit had been left behind in the old homes. We had good neighbours, but not close neighbours.

Nonetheless, there were huge benefits. We had a decent-sized garden, albeit heavy clay that would have been good for making bricks. We had electricity throughout the house; we had an indoor and outdoor toilet, but most significant of all was the indoor bathroom. Oh, great joy. It took over a month for the novelty to wear off, turning on the taps and pulling out the plug. Best of all was being right on the edge of the countryside. At the bottom of our garden was a hedge and beyond that fields of dairy cattle and cider orchards. These became our playgrounds. Over the years, the town has pushed its boundaries outwards and those fields have gone, with just one cider orchard remaining from the dozen or so of my youth.

From that day on, through the rest of my childhood, we spent the daylight hours in the wilds of the country, and the hours of darkness walking on the wild side on one of the largest council estates in the West Country. The contrast could not have been greater. Wild young town lads from a council estate pushed up against the tranquillity of the countryside. It was a clash of cultures with an ugly as well as a bright side. It introduced me to wildlife, initially as a young egg collector but later as a young naturalist. For others, it provided the opportunities for sports which were cruel in the extreme.

I will never forget one family whose children were more evil than most. At school, they were the ones no one wanted to play with. Outside of school, they had some sick ideas of entertainment. One of them found sport in using an air-rifle to shoot out the eyes of the dairy cattle in the nearby fields. Lots of us had air-rifles and would take a shot at rabbits or wood pigeons, but they were in a different league. Many of them were later to spend time at Her Majesty's pleasure.

Split the Kipper

The estate housed a population of around 6,000 working-class people and that inevitably brought its problems. At night, as I said, we roamed the estate as gangs, not like today's gangs, but in smaller groups of perhaps four or five. Everybody carried knives, usually openly displayed in a sheath on the trouser belt. There were no knife laws until I was about 13 years old when flick-knives were made illegal in the wake of a spate of Teddy Boy stabbings. We used large sheath knives to play a game of chicken called 'Split the Kipper'. All you needed to play this game was the large knife, soft ground, a stout pair of shoes and a good deal of stupidity. It was a game for two, each with his own knife. The two of you would stand about a yard apart, facing each other with your feet close together, as though standing to attention. You took it in turns to be first to go and the first player would throw his knife aiming it at the ground just to the left or right of the opponent's feet. The idea is that your opponent must then move his foot out to where the knife lands so that gradually after a number of throws, his feet are so far apart that he falls over.

The knife had to stick in the ground or the throw didn't count. To keep the game fair, it also had to land within a hand span of the opponent's foot and not two yards away. Players took it in turns to throw. When your legs were far apart, you could return to your original position if you 'Split the Kipper'. To do this, you had to throw your knife and make it stick anywhere between your opponent's feet. This was fairly easy when his legs were wide apart but not if they were close together. This is where the stout pair of shoes and the stupidity came in. Basically the way the game progressed was that you would gradually get your legs further and further apart until one player split the kipper. Then it got interesting. His feet would be put so close together that it was almost impossible to get a knife between them, but that was the only way the opponent stood a chance of getting back into the game. We played this game for hours and we still have all our original toes!

There would be the odd punch up between rival groups but these tended to be between individuals rather than gang on gang. That came at a higher level. There were two major estates in the town, Hamp and Sydenham, plus the lesser one of Newtown. The real rivalry existed between the Hamp and the Sydenham lads. In a nutshell, you kept away from each other's areas. We may have had the occasional inter-gang conflict on our own estate but those rivalries were put to one side if someone from Hamp came onto our patch, and vice versa. One memorable episode that sticks in my mind was when friend and neighbour Roy got into a spot of bother at the town's YMCA. One of his friends was about to get picked on by a group of well-known trouble-makers, brothers as it happened. Roy knew it would end in a fight and, being outnumbered, decided he should get in a few punches while he could. Nonetheless, he was significantly outnumbered and took a bit of a beating. When he got home, he got a right rollicking from his mother, not for fighting but for getting blood on his new shirt!

Fifty years on, the culture of inter-estate rivalry has changed very little. If a youth activity was introduced to encourage youngsters to get together, and it was put on the Sydenham Estate, Hamp youngsters would not attend, and likewise if it was a Hamp-based activity. To be successful, it would need to be in the town centre, neutral territory. This even applies at adult level. Very few people from one estate would attend an event of the other, but they'd all go to a town centre event and mix without knowing it. And so the two estates each had their own and separate community centres. On the Sydenham estate, it all began in an old Nissen hut, a remnant of the war years. Eventually it grew into a quite decent community centre which has survived the test of time and still flourishes. Conveniently it was, and remains, next to the chip shop and neighbouring block of shops and hence has always been the place where youngsters gather.

Rites of passage

It was during this time that we were 'coming of age'. Street credibility was everything. In our eyes, to be a man, first you had to smoke. Everybody smoked in our gang and had done so since about the age of eleven. We would earn money to buy cheap cigarettes and it was much easier in those days to buy them, even when you were well under age. If questioned, you would just say that they were for your dad. There were shops which sold cigarettes individually or would split a packet for you, clearly catering for the underage market.

Dave and I decided to set up our own trading company, buying and selling cigarettes. We bought loose tobacco and made roll-ups. It was moderately successful but took a rather devious course at one stage when we were aged about twelve. We were kicking our heels in the street and spotted a particularly long dog-end, still with a good bit of tobacco in it. It was then that we realised we could reduce the overheads associated with raw materials by recycling dog-ends, as long as no one spotted us collecting them. We were, of course, more than conscious of the hygiene issues and so, in fairness to our regular customers, we washed and dried the tobacco first before blending it with fresh material. Our most regular customers were two brothers who went wild over our new brand, much milder than what they had experienced before. The business died a death when the council introduced road-sweepers. As thirteen-year-old entrepreneurs, we had experienced our first taste of external market forces.

Cigarettes had other, more adventurous, uses – discovering girls. Girlfriends seemed to come and go, often just one-night stands as we entered our early teens and adventured into journeys of discovery. The girls on the estate, at least those that were allowed out at night, were all rated according to 'grope ability'. We knew the rankings of the regular girls and were all aware when any progression was made up the league table. As lads, it was normal to boast of having reached one or two places higher up the table than was the reality. As we grew older, so the relationships became more stable.

Christine was a friend who went to the girls' grammar school while I was attending the boys' grammar. She was perhaps a bit more adventurous than most and one evening, she was in the back of a car down a country lane enjoying the company of her new boyfriend. So engrossed were they that they failed to hear the village bobby as he approached silently on his push bike. Seeing a car in a gated field entrance, he decided to investigate and shone his torch through the steamy windows. Christine was horrified when she recognised the policeman's voice. 'Oh, it's you, Christine. Thought I'd found an abandoned car. Give my regards to your dad!' and off he went. He was her father's best friend!

We were now at an age, fifteen or so, where we would go further afield in our search for female friendship and would venture to the neighbouring villages and towns. Dave and I at the time were courting a couple of girls from North Petherton and this meant that we spent less time with each other and more alone with the girls. The North Petherton lads took a dislike to our presence in the village and we fell victims to a fast and furious punch-up. It was six of them against two of us. The long-term result of this was two loose front teeth which I was later to lose. However, when we got back into town, we related what had happened, telling a friend whose family was in farming and lived in a nearby village. The friend said, 'No problem. I'll get the lads to sort them out.' We tried to convince him that there was no need; it was best forgotten. It was no use. Some of those young farmers loved a scrap, especially if it was with the North Petherton boys. We found out later that several Land Rovers full of young farmers descended on North Petherton and redressed the balance.

We also used to catch the train to Weston-Super-Mare, which was the main attraction on a summer's bank holiday. This was during the period when the Mods and Rockers were mortal enemies, the Mods with their scooters and trendy clothes, the Rockers with their motorbikes and black leather wear. One bank holiday weekend, there was the mother and father of a punch-up between the two rival groups at Weston. Although we belonged to neither fraternity, we all knew what was going to happen. The Mods and Rockers came from far and wide, mostly Bristol, London and the Midlands. There were scores of arrests but no local lads amongst them. This was surprising because the orchestration of this well-planned event was the brainchild of a Bridgwater gang leader, the one from the other side of the town to us. The police knew who was to blame but it could never be proven.

That sinking feeling

The best time to visit Weston or Burnham-on-Sea was at low tide, mid-afternoon on a Bank Holiday Monday. The tide goes out a long way, about two miles, and gives the illusion of a long and wide sandy beach, where you can drive out a considerable distance towards the sea. It's not so. The sea goes out such a long way because the slope of the beach is almost imperceptible. When the tide comes in, because the slope is so shallow, it comes in almost as fast as you can retreat away from it. Normally standing on a shore line anywhere else, you will be aware of the waves lapping around your feet, but with such a shallow gradient on the Somerset coast, you don't realise that the tide is coming in under the sand well before you see it coming in above the sand. That mix of sand and water creates quicksand. Before you know it, you're going down. The locals understand this but the young lads from the Midlands had no idea. So, Bank Holiday sport on a summer's day when the tide was out was watching the Brummies drive up and down the beach, showing off to their girls, gradually going further and further out until the wheels inexplicably sank in the sand. Once it starts, there's no going back. It's like a fly in a spider's web; the more it struggles, the more entangled it becomes. Then imagine another fly comes to help. That too becomes trapped. That's Weston beach when the conditions are perfect.

On one such weekend, we watched four Birmingham lads fall foul of the quicksand. One of them got out of the car and ran back up the beach to get help. He went to a big white van that was with their group and persuaded the driver to go out with a tow-rope. This he did and like the second spider in the web, he too was ensnared. By now the first car had sunk so deep that the doors could not be opened and the passengers had to climb out through the windows. We watched as the car slowly sank as the tide came in to finish the job. Then the van went the same way. The driver escaped and ran back up the beach and watched in disbelief as his beloved van was devoured by the incoming tide. It sank into the sand up to its wheel arches and then the sea took over. When the waves reached up to bonnet level, the sea water crept in and completed every electrical circuit. You could hear a muffled 'beep, beep' from the horn as the four orange warning lights on the corners of the roof pulsed their amber flashes. As the waves finally engulfed the entire vehicle, the last evidence of its presence was four amber-pulsing orbs, like fluorescent jellyfish just below the surface. The following morning, there was no evidence of its previous existence, now deep in the sand. There must be hundreds of cars beneath those beaches which were once the pride and joy of the London and Midland lads.

The final steady girlfriend

My spell in the sixth form only lasted six months. I have always been impatient by nature and need to be kept busy. I found that of the 35 lesson periods per week, I only had to attend 15 of them. Twenty periods were available for private study. I was getting bored and decided that

The Odeon cinema in Bridgwater where I enjoyed my first date with Lorna.

what I needed to learn, I could do at night school and meanwhile I could go to work and earn some money. I was still just sixteen years old but it paid off. I passed my 'A' levels a year earlier than I would have done if I had stayed at the grammar school, and I met a new girlfriend, Lorna, who later became my wife. It was my life-long friend Dave who introduced us. He was already going out with another girl on the same secretarial course as Lorna.

Our first date was a trip to the cinema. There were two cinemas in the town at that time, the Palace and the Odeon. They were right across the road from each other. I had planned to go to see the film at the Palace but Lorna's bus was due to arrive outside the Odeon. She duly stepped off the bus and I must have been so nervous that instead of going across the road to the Palace, I went straight into the Odeon. We watched a war movie instead of the romantic *South Pacific!*

A week later, it was Valentine's Day and early in the morning, I dropped a highly-perfumed Valentine's card through her letter box and quietly slipped away unnoticed. When I visited her that evening, no mention was made of the card. The tradition with Valentine cards was not to sign them with your name so I simply signed it as 'Guess who'. That evening, the lack of mention of the card left me wandering if she had so many other boyfriends that she couldn't guess which one it was from. As the evening progressed, I grew increasingly anxious about the unspoken question until I could hold back no longer, and then the story unfolded. Lorna was the eldest of nine children, six of them sisters. The family also had a mongrel dog named Timmy. It transpired that when I put the card through the letter box, the dog found the perfumed card irresistible and ate it. All that remained was chewed-up papier-mâché. Not only could they not read the card but nor could they read the envelope to determine which of the nine siblings it was for. It was the last Valentine's card that I ever sent!

Timmy was to cause me further grief. During our courting years, we never seemed to be able to get out of the house very early, so we looked for an acceptable reason to escape and we offered to take Timmy for a walk. Just a few minutes away was a country lane and we headed down that to find a field gate where we tied up the dog and continued with our courting. Unfortunately, we were paying more attention to each other than to the dog. He had clearly got fed up waiting and chewed through his lead. When we returned to pick him up, there was about four inches of lead hanging from the gate and no dog to be found. When we got home, Timmy was already there ahead of us. I apologised to my girlfriend's father for the late return, blaming it on the dog and claiming that he had pulled so hard on his lead that he had snapped it. Whether or not he believed my story, I never discovered but the following night he asked us to walk the dog and presented us with a new lead – made of metal chain.

By now I had begun a new period of my life. My childhood was over. I had left school, started work and was courting. I had entered the adults' world where a new set of adventures and memorable encounters awaited me, sufficient on their own to merit a sequel to this chapter of my life. Watch this space – perhaps I'll call it *Last of the Somerset Wine!*

Other titles by Roger Evans
published by Countryside Books

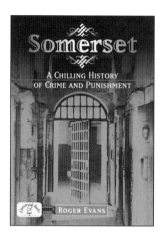

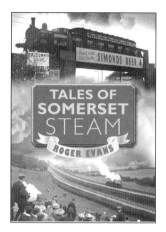

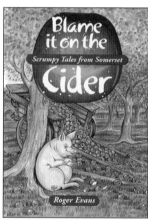

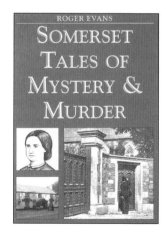